Copyright © 2024 Stephanie Lee Villafranca

All rights reserved

No part of this book may be reproduced, or stored in a retrieval system, or transmitted in any form or by any means, electronic, mechanical, photocopying, recording, or otherwise, without express written permission of the publisher except as permitted by U.S. copyright law.

This publication is designed to provide accurate and authoritative information in regard to the subject matter covered. It is sold with the understanding that neither the author nor the publisher is engaged in rendering legal or professional services. While the publisher and author have used their best efforts in preparing this book, they make no representations or warranties with respect to the accuracy or completeness of the contents of this book and specifically disclaim any implied warranties of merchantability or fitness for a particular purpose. No warranty may be created or extended by sales representatives or written sales materials. The advice and strategies contained herein may not be suitable for your situation. You should consult with a professional when appropriate. Neither the publisher nor the author shall be liable for any loss or any damages, including but not limited to special, incidental, consequential, personal, or other damages.

ISBN-13: 9798321248485
ISBN-10: 1477123456

Cover design by: Stephanie Lee Villafrancar
Library of Congress Control Number: 2018675309
Printed in the United States of America

Love is patient,
Love is kind.
It does not envy,
It does not boast,
It is not proud.
It is not rude,
It is not self-seeking,
It is not easily angered,
It keeps no record of wrongs.
Love does not delight in evil
But rejoices with the truth.
It always protects,
Always trusts,
Always hopes,
Always perseveres.
Love never fails.
I Corinthians 13:4-8a

Keypers

Keys to Finding and Keeping Pure Love

*by
Stephanie Villafranca*

Table of Contents

Chapter 1 -- Purity
Chapter 2 -------------------- Love is God Because God is Love
Chapter 3 ------------------------------ Purity in Relationships
Chapter 4 -- Love is Patient
Chapter 5 -- Love is Kind
Chapter 6 ---------------------------------- Love Does Not Envy
Chapter 7 ----------------- Love Does Not Boast/Is not Proud
Chapter 8 -------------------------------------- Love is Not Rude
Chapter 9 ---------------------------- Love is Not Self Seeking
Chapter 10 ----------------------- Love is Not Easily Angered
Chapter 11 --------------------- Love Does Not Delight in Evil
Chapter 12 --------------------- Love Rejoices With the Truth
Chapter 13 ------------------------------ Love Always Protects
Chapter 14 -------------------------------- Love Always Trusts
Chapter 15 -------------------------------- Love Always Hopes
Chapter 16 -------------------------- Love Always Perseveres
Chapter 17 ----------------------------------- Love Never Fails

About the Author and Acknowledgments

My name is Stephanie Villafranca. I'm a lover of Jesus and believe that the Bible is His love letter to us and a guide for our lives. I'm the wife of a wonderful pastor who loves God and works hard to provide for our family in every way. I'm the mother of two amazing and spunky children who have strong and unique personalities, and a beautiful, kind, and selfless older daughter through marriage who has been such an amazing example of God's redeeming grace within our family.

I grew up in a broken home. My single mom raised my brother and me to the best of her ability. She worked hard to provide for our needs and give us a strong education both scholastically and spiritually. Our church family helped to raise my brother and me. Our small church also served as our school. I had quite the supportive community when I was young. I will always be grateful for the teachers, youth leaders, friends, pastors, and authority figures who helped me to navigate my teen years.

My mom was my biggest influence. She taught me how to love God with all my heart, soul, mind, and strength. She taught me integrity, purity, and good work ethic. She gave me a passion for music and using my musical ability to bring honor to God. She pushed me to do things I was not confident in my ability to do and encouraged me to use the talents God gave me for His glory. She taught me to love people and serve without expecting anything in return. She taught me to see people for where they are in life and for who God made them to be. She was forgiving, gracious, and kind, as well as firm and uncompromising in her convictions and faith.

One of her greatest gifts to me was the gift of understanding why God requests me to live a life of purity. She instilled in me the desire to please God by keeping my heart and mind pure. Because of this, I knew that if I was obedient and faithful to Him,

He would be faithful to bring the perfect husband for me - A man who loves God and takes his rightful place as head of our house in the most loving and caring way - A man who loves me the way Christ loves the church.

Because of my mom, I can write this book with full confidence that if you follow the truths written within these pages you will have the tools you need to discover God's plan for your life which is worth more than you could ever think or imagine.

This book is dedicated to and in honor of my mom

- Patricia Sarah Gatewood

Purity

Chapter 1

Purity - Noun: "freedom from immorality, especially of a sexual nature"

My Story

I am a Keyper. I saved sex for marriage. I will never regret that decision. A decision not made lightly or at the spur of the moment, but a value system set in place by God and nurtured by my mom.

It was Valentine's Day, 1990, and I was 7 years old. My mom had been working with teen girls at our church teaching them about purity. She called it the "Key Club" and had written a curriculum to help the girls understand the importance of purity and saving themselves for marriage. I frequently went to the meetings with her and played or colored in the other room, but she was pretty sure I was hearing at least some of the conversations, so she decided it was time to give me "the talk." You know, the one all parents dread and every child is embarrassed to talk about.

But my mom made that day special for us. We went to a park where she explained the science and biology of our bodies, sex, and how babies are made. Afterwards, she explained to me that sex is something that is special between husband and wife and should be saved for marriage. She told me that until the day I get married, God should hold the key to my heart (the very reason behind the name "Key Club"). My 7-year-old mind somehow comprehended the concept, and I accepted my first promise ring from my mom. She had designed the beautiful ring and had it made for the "Key Club." It consisted of a heart with a cross in the middle, and the heart was the handle to a key. I cherished that ring for many years, and when I grew out of it, I got a larger one. I wish I could say I still have my first ring, but I am excited to say that after many years of not knowing where I put the second ring, I finally found it! I may not have been able to keep close tabs on my many purity rings, but I am proud that I always had one, along with the resolve that I would save myself for the man I would marry.

"Why does God care about my purity?"

Many people think that God is some distant being who set the world in motion and set up a bunch of rules to keep us under control. Nothing can be further from the truth! God is deeply interested in every aspect of our lives. He wants us to be happy, healthy, and well-rounded people with lots of friends and good strong relationships. I want to show you that God's idea of saving sex for marriage isn't to make things hard on you. He's not just tacking on more rules because He wants to be obeyed. He has very specific and important reasons for asking us to hold off on the most intimate and special act that can be expressed between a husband and wife. The real reason is because He wants you to have a joyful and fulfilling life, and He knows that if you follow His plan for marriage, you'll have the best shot at a long and happy marriage.

To achieve His goals, God set up guidelines for us to live by so that we won't ruin it for ourselves. But what do we do? We ruin it for ourselves ... over and over again. We've taken His gift of free will and turned it against our own well-being by doing what feels good "in the moment" and putting temporary pleasure ahead of ... well, everything.

"Well, that's cool for you. But what does it have to do with me?"

You may think that purity sounds like a novel idea. A sweet

thought, but not very realistic. The whole point is to make it to your wedding day without having sex. Why bother? It's just sex. Everyone is doing it. It doesn't really mean anything ... does it? Once you're married, you've fulfilled the "purity pledge" and it's all over, right? What's the point, really? And why have you written a whole book on the subject when the point is simple? ... "Don't have sex until marriage or God will smite you!"

Let's set this straight right now. First, God is not going to smite you if you have sex before marriage. Second, Purity isn't just saving sex for marriage. Purity is so much more! It's living a life pleasing to God. It's making sure that what you look at, listen to, eat, drink, who you hang out with, where you go, and what you do are good for you in the short term and in the long run. Living a pure life will show your love for God, your appreciation of His love for you, and your love for others.

> *Finally, brothers and sisters, whatever is true, whatever is noble, whatever is right, whatever is pure, whatever is lovely, whatever is admirable—if anything is excellent or praiseworthy—think about such things.*
> *Philippians 4:8*

Think about it this way... if you put black ink into a pen, black ink will come out. If you put red ink into a pen, red ink will come out. In the same way, what you put into your life will determine what comes out of it.

Purity is designed to help us achieve a life without regrets. Regrets like:
  - Saying things we shouldn't have said
  - Doing things we shouldn't have done
  - Saying "yes" to someone when we should have said "no."

- Getting too close to that toxic person
- Seeing that thing that we wish we had never seen and now can't get out of our head
- Being involved in that relationship and giving our all to it just to have it not work out
- Allowing ourselves to be taken in by that person who used us and abused us
- Getting into a toxic or loveless relationship
- Wasting our time, energy, affection, and attention on that person who wasn't putting the same amount of work into the relationship

Purity will help you see the red flags clearly so that you can avoid a lot of heartache. Purity will help you see the road signs that lead to fully understanding what true love really looks like. The purpose of waiting for marriage is not to deprive you of love, affection, or fun. If it's to deprive you of anything, it's to deprive you of regret, pain, loneliness, irreversible damage, and a broken heart.

The goal here is not to take away your fun, but to help you find a whole new level of fun! I want to help you learn how to dream about your future, prepare for your wedding, set yourself up for success, give yourself the best shot at finding your best match, and have fun doing it! The goal is to elevate your idea of sex from recreation to a pure and beautiful expression of God's love for you and your future spouse, and your love for each other.

You are more precious than a truckload of diamonds, and your purity is something that has more value than you may realize. Only you can decide to keep it or give it away. If you decide to keep or regain your purity, I would like to give you the tools you'll need to keep it safe for the rest of your life. Even after you're married.

Within the pages of this book, you will discover what real love looks like. I want to help you to unravel the lies that society puts on relationships and break down the expectations society sets up for your sexuality.

> *"So, what's the big deal? Why would I want to become a Keyper? I mean, saving sex for marriage is so old fashioned. Times have changed since a few decades ago, and sex is just fun and doesn't mean anything."*

...That's what society would like you to think, anyway.

Most people have been led to believe that it is strange to be pure, and very odd to save sex for marriage. But nothing could be further from the truth! God designed sex as a wonderful experience to be shared only between a husband and wife.

Society will tell you that sex is, "no big deal," or "it's just something fun to do." But too many people have felt guilty, dirty, taken advantage of, hurt, unloved, or ugly after giving their virginity away. Many have gotten Sexually Transmitted Diseases (STDs) that have changed their lives forever because they or their significant other did not stick to one partner. And of course still others have ended up with an unexpected pregnancy. That is because sex was not designed to be used this way! Most of those people have had to put up walls around their hearts or turn off their emotions to keep having sex, denying that anything seems "off," but knowing full well something is missing.

If you've been there before, part of you knows what I'm talking about. Sex is a big deal. It's a lot bigger deal than society makes it out to be. Why do they downplay it? Perhaps it's to make themselves feel better about decisions they have made. You see, God designed sex as a beautiful pleasurable, and fun (yes - fun), act to be enjoyed between husband and wife. It's designed to help husband and wife become closer together in intimacy, and also for the purpose of creating more life. Believe it or not, sexual intimacy was also designed by God to help us understand Him more deeply! There are many reasons why God designed sex only for marriage. ALL of them work back to His immeasurable love for you and His desire for your life to be blessed in ways you can only imagine.

While it can be momentarily fun and exciting to have sex with someone you are not married to, there are innumerable consequences that are unforeseeable at the time. The most obvious are risk of pregnancy or STDs. Making the decision to wait for marriage drastically cuts your chances of contracting one of many STDs. If you have not heard much about STDs, I encourage you to find someone to talk to who can go through all the STDs, the risks, symptoms, and anything else you can learn about them. You may have heard quite enough about STDs in school (or if you had an over informative mom like mine), and because it's a subject that could have its own book, I won't elaborate on it here.

The not so obvious consequences lie beneath the surface ... in the mind and heart. Those are the ones I would like to unwrap for you.

One of my favorite reasons for saving sex for marriage is cutting down on the risk of bad or broken relationships. If you make it clear from the very beginning that sex is not going to happen while you're dating, I guarantee you that the "bad apples" will run for the hills before you even have a chance to get emotionally invested. Some will even agree with your rules at first but will take off when they finally realize that you're serious. Usually, they say something to the effect of, "We can take it as slow as you want." Which is code for, "I'll be patient for now, but I'm sure you don't REALLY mean to wait until you're married. You just want to feel more comfortable with our relationship first."

If you start having sex right away in a relationship, you will honestly never know if your partner loves you for who you are, or just for what you are willing to put out. You also won't know if you love your partner for who he is because you have not tested the most intensely passionate part of his being. His sexual self-control.

God created a better plan. Pure love allows you to skip the heartache and pain of giving away your virginity to the wrong person. His plan is for you to keep your purity safe and well cared for until you can give it to someone who will also keep your purity safe and well cared for.

One of the beautiful things about this gift is that if you save your purity for your husband, you will never have to give it up! When you share that precious gift with your husband, the gift becomes something you and your husband get to share forever.

Try to grasp this concept. Purity doesn't stop at marriage. Yes, you read that right. Married couples are pure when they keep their focus on God and remain faithful to each other.

Not having sex before marriage provides you a measure of protection from the extra emotional turmoil that happens when you break up with someone after you have been physically united with them. When you have sex with someone, you have given them the most physical vulnerability you have to offer. When you break up, you can't take that back like you can your favorite hoodie or hat. There is already enough emotional pain to work through after a breakup. Do you really want to add on more pain than you must?

Saving sex for marriage teaches both of you self-control. Let me tell you, self-control is one of the most important things for you to have in a relationship. When you are arguing with each other, you need self-control to not name call or go off on each other. When you become a parent, self-control is incredibly important to raise happy and emotionally healthy children. You even need self-control to be able to manage finances as a couple. If you can learn how to be self-controlled with your body before you get married, you have a solid foundation for self-control in your marriage and throughout the rest of your life.

When you have sex before you're married, there is a sense that everything is fine, that you both love each other, and that you'll be together forever. As nice as it sounds, it's actually a smoke screen. Refusing to have sex until you're married draws out the worst and most intense emotions in both of you. I know it doesn't sound appealing but trust me it is a VERY good thing. This means that before your relationship becomes physical, and before you become too emotionally invested in the relationship, you will both find out who the other person really is ... the good, the bad, and the ugly. After you find out who you are and who your partner is, you will be able to clearly decide on whether or not you really want to spend the rest of your life with that person.

If you're not having sex, you are forced to resolve conflict using your emotions and your intellect instead of your body. You've seen it in the movies. The couple is arguing with each other. Tensions rise as they are pouring out all their pent-up frustrations to each other. One of them finally grabs the other and steals a passionate kiss. The other is silenced and so shocked by the move that all the anger is gone, and everything is ok. In many of these scenarios, the couple moves into a night of passionate sex which erases all misgivings and resolves all issues. Cute thought.

While this makes for great storytelling, it is unrealistic in so many ways, but many people try to resolve conflict by having sex to distract from the issue. This is not healthy. All it does is sweep the problem under the rug until the next time it rears its ugly head. I can tell you without a shadow of a doubt that there are many issues that people don't work through when they've had sex before marriage or moved in together. They end up either having to deal with those things after they are already committed and financially dependent on each other or never deal with them at all and end up either miserable or divorced. I can confidently say that if they had taken the time to work through those issues at the beginning of their relationship, they would be happier, and their relationship would be more stable.

If you do not have sex (and especially if you do not move in together), you both have an "easy out" of the relationship. Think about it. If you both have the freedom to walk away at any moment, and you stick it out through the good times and the bad, you have a solid foundation upon which to build a good and lasting relationship.

Not having sex before marriage brings you to a deep level of respect for each other. You will need to learn each other's personal boundaries and be able to back off if one or both of you is becoming a little too sexually aroused. When you can learn respect for each other at this intensity, it will be easier to learn respect for each other in other ways throughout your relationship.

Saving sex for marriage also proves that you are putting the interests of your future children before your need for immediate satisfaction. If your birth control fails and you end up having children before you are married, you run a much higher risk of spending your life in a loveless relationship "for the sake of the kids," splitting up, ending up with custody battles, child support issues, and lack of stability. Some of you already know what it's like to be the child in homes like this. Do you really want that for your future children?

Even if you already have kids, you can decide from this point on to save all future sex until you're married. Not only will you still get all the benefits of waiting until marriage, you will set a solid example for your kids to follow. As your kids get older, you should have honest conversations with them about why you decided to wait until marriage to have sex again. Your example is the most effective reason for them to make the same decision for themselves. As a bonus, you will also be able to influence siblings, nieces, nephews, and any other children in your life to do the same.

If you are a virgin and have decided to wait, you have the advantage of bringing much less baggage into future relationships and marriage. You and your future spouse won't have to think about the fact that you've had sex with someone else. You won't have to worry about comparing past relationships or sexual experiences with your current spouse. How nice would that be?

If you have already had sex in the past but have decided that you are going to wait from this point forward, you will be putting more distance between past experiences and your future relationship, which will allow more time for feelings and memories to fade. You'll be able to enter your marriage on a fresh new page. If you make the decision for purity now, you can draw a kind of "line in the sand." You can say, everything before this point was someone else. This is the new me that is working toward a solid and healthy future relationship.

Determining to wait until your wedding day, will not only give you a sense of accomplishment, it will also make your wedding night that much more special and "magical."

Does this mean that people that have sex before marriage are doomed to have ruined relationships, or will never be satisfied?

And does it mean that if you do wait, your marriage is never going to fall apart? I won't lie to you. The truth is that nothing is guaranteed. It is possible for people to have sex before marriage and still end up married and with a good relationship, and even couples who wait to have sex until they are married can end up splitting in the end. It's more about risk and odds. The odds of finding a good solid relationship with someone who is willing to put the time and the effort into investing into your relationship are far higher than with someone who is in the relationship because "it feels right" or "we are in love." On the other hand, your risk of ending up in a bad relationship increases if you get into a relationship without really getting to know one another on a deep friendship and intellectual level first.

Could this person that you're having sex with really be the man of your dreams? Could you really get married and live happily ever after? The chances are slim. Yes, it happens but rarely. Please don't fool yourself into thinking that your relationship (which started outside of God's guidelines) will be one of the unlikely exceptions to the overwhelming statistics of broken hearts and relationships. Even if you do end up getting married, and managing to make your relationship work, it will be much harder for the two of you to work through your differences, and the reason is because you clouded those issues as soon as you put sexual intimacy into the mix.

But this book isn't even about sex! I realize that might be counter-intuitive considering this whole first chapter discussed sex, but the thing is that purity in relationships is so much deeper than that. The truth is that more broken relationships come out of a lack of a true understanding of what pure love is. THAT is what I want to bring to the table. A chance at pure love.

Love is God – Because God is Love

Chapter 2

"Dear friends, let us love one another, for love comes from God. Everyone who loves has been born of God and knows God. Whoever does not love does not know God, because God is love."

I John 4:7-8

Hang with me here. I may start to sound like I'm getting off subject. But I promise that within this chapter is the foundation of everything I've ever learned about real love. In order to understand love completely, we need to start at the source. God is Love. Love comes from God. Without God, pure love cannot exist. So, in this chapter, I want to tell you God's love story for the world.

Pure Love

At the beginning, God decided to create everything we know as the universe. He wanted to create something He could be proud of. He did an amazing job creating the universe, light, earth, land, water, fish, plants, animals, and birds. But it wasn't enough. He wanted to share this amazing creation with someone. So, He created man and named him Adam; a part of himself placed into flesh to love and fellowship with Him. He gave Adam charge of His creation to care for and to explore. He taught Adam to use the tools and resources available in creation to be creative and build. He gave him charge of the animals to care for and name. Everything was good. It was a paradise we could enjoy without regret.

Here's the beauty of pure love. God did not want Adam to mindlessly obey and serve Him. He wanted Adam to decide whether or not to love Him! He wanted to fellowship with him knowing that it was his decision to love Him back. So, He gave Adam a choice. And it was more than just a choice to obey or disobey. What he gave him was far more powerful. The option to understand the difference between good and evil. He could live on earth and enjoy creation only knowing the Goodness of God, or his eyes could be opened to the realities of evil and it would then birth evil in Adam. So, God placed a tree in the middle of the Garden of Eden and told Adam not to eat any of its fruit. He called it the Tree of the Knowledge of Good and Evil, and told him that if he ate of it, he would die. Not that it was a physical poison that would kill him immediately, but that the decision to eat the fruit would be an act of disobedience which would break trust between God and man. This would cause Adam to be separated from God… the Giver of life. Sin would take root in Adam's heart which would bring death and destruction into the world.

After giving Adam the responsibility of caring for his creation, God decided to find him a helper. A companion who would be by his side to care for the earth and the animals. But there was nothing in all of creation that was good enough to fulfill that role in Adam's life. So, God made Adam fall asleep and did something incredible. He took one of Adam's ribs and used it to form Adam's perfect companion. A woman named Eve. She was Adam's equal in value for she was a part of his very flesh. But she was different. She was his perfect match. God had taken his masculine nature and placed it in Adam. He placed his feminine nature into Eve. Together, they formed the fullness of God's personality. A complete image of who God is. Now, together they would be able to care perfectly for God's creation.

Love Does not Boast/Is not Proud

But something else was happening that Adam did not know about. You see, God had made angels...ministering spirits to do His will and be messengers for Him. One of these angels was called Lucifer. His name means "star of the morning" and he was beautiful and powerful. He was considered wise and good until pride settled in his heart. He decided that he was so beautiful and glorious that he should be worshiped like God. He rebelled against God and convinced one third of the angels to rebel with him. His pride was his downfall, and he was cast out of Heaven. That's when he turned his attention on us. The crown of God's creation. If he could corrupt us, not only would he exact revenge on God, but he would also gain more followers to feed his ego and make him feel more powerful than God.

Love Does not Envy

But creation was so wonderful! Adam and Eve had everything they could ever want or need. They had beautiful fellowship with God who would come every day to spend time with them. What reason could they possibly have to turn their backs on God? Lucifer had to be creative, cunning, and convincing. He used the one thing that God had forbidden them to do in order to entice them to disobey God. Lucifer convinced Eve to eat fruit from the Tree of the Knowledge of Good and Evil. He pointed out how beautiful the fruit was and how wonderful it must taste. He deceived her into thinking that God was just trying to keep them from becoming like Himself and that eating the fruit would give her wisdom.

Love is Not Self Seeking

So, Eve ate the fruit and then turned to her husband who was standing right there with her and convinced him to eat it as well. Life as they knew it was suddenly changed. Their disobedience birthed sin in their hearts. The trust between God and humans was broken. When God asked Adam about it, Adam blamed Eve. Trust between man and woman was broken. When God asked Eve about it, Eve blamed Lucifer and they became enemies.

God had made the universe and given us the responsibility to rule over it. What a gift! But we turned around and gave ownership of the world over to Lucifer and gave him the power to rule over us. Spiritual and physical death had entered the world. Satan had exacted his revenge on God and had gained power over God's creation.

Love Does Not Delight in Evil

God had to remove Adam and Eve from the Garden of Eden so that they could not eat from the Tree of Life and live forever with this separation from Himself. So, Adam and Eve had to leave their home and learn how to live and survive in a world which was no longer perfect. Adam had to work the ground and fight with weeds in order to make fruits and vegetables grow for he and his wife to eat. Eve would be subject to her husband and giving birth would now be a painful experience. The animals began to turn on each other, and instead of all creatures eating plants, some started to eat flesh.

Love is Patient

But God refused to leave it like this. This was not the end of the story. He still loved His creation. Adam and Eve were still precious to Him. A plan had to be set into motion to remove sin from the hearts of humans and allow for us to return to fellowship with God. But how? A sinless God cannot be in perfect fellowship with sinful people. He cannot stand by and watch us hurt and destroy each other. He had to make a way to fix it. But there was nothing on Earth that could redeem us, and we could not do it for ourselves.

God would have to become flesh in order to redeem us. So, He planned out the perfect time in history to come as a child. To be birthed to a woman which started the healing process between His Majesty and women who had been so easily deceived to disobey Him. So, God took a part of Himself and became flesh. God the Son entered the world. His name is Jesus.

Jesus grew and became a child who went through all the same ups and downs children have to face. He dealt with bumps and bruises, making friends, and losing them. He may have been teased or bullied from time to time. He had to learn to read and write. He obeyed his earthly parents and honored God the Father throughout His childhood.

Love Always Perseveres

When He became a man, Jesus went for a time into the wilderness to spend time with His Father God and prepare for His ministry to us here on Earth. Lucifer took the opportunity of his solitude to test and tempt Him. For 40 days, Jesus was tested and tempted to sin. He faced every temptation that we face and was bombarded by them one after another. Maybe He even wondered if He would go crazy! At the end of his 40 days, Lucifer tempted him with 3 specific things. His hunger, His safety, and pride. In the end, after Jesus had resisted every temptation Satan threw at him, he offered Him power over the physical kingdoms of the earth. But Jesus knew better. This battle was not about his health, his physical body, or any physical kingdom. He shot truth back at Satan and refused to cave to fleshly desires. He had been tested, and He had been found worthy to redeem God's people back to Himself.

"For God so loved the world that he gave his one and only Son, that whoever believes in him shall not perish but have eternal life."
John 3:16

Love is Kind

His ministry to people on Earth started. Healing between God and man could begin. He called 12 men to become his most intimate disciples. He taught multitudes and healed many from mental and physical ailments. He brought spiritual healing to many who had wandered away from their faith in God. He took authority over the fallen angels who were wreaking havoc on earth and in people's lives. God's kingdom which had been taken from us was slowly starting to shine through Jesus and his followers.

But the people still did not fully understand what was going on. The promised Savior that they had been waiting for had come, but not in the way they expected. They thought that He was coming to overthrow human governments and establish His Kingdom over the Jews here on Earth. But God's plan was much bigger and much deeper than that. Sin had entered this world and permeated every part of it. His plan was to come and redeem His people and then to build for them a new home when this life had run its course.

Love is not Rude

Jesus kept healing and feeding people. He kept teaching them about goodness and kindness. He defied human laws to show us a better way and to grow God's law of love in our hearts. You see, we had been given laws to govern us and keep us from hurting ourselves and others. These were the 10 commandments. Then, those who loved power added on to those laws. Over many years, law was stacked on top of law until there was no way any human could ever follow them. The teachers of the law thought they were doing well, but pride had arisen in most of their hearts, and they used their knowledge and position to rule over the people.

Jesus taught a simpler way. He cut through the clutter and brought it back to basics. The 10 commandments. He simplified it even more by breaking it all the way down to 2 things. Love God and love others. If we truly love God, we will follow Him and obey Him. We won't want to do anything that disappoints Him, hurts Him, or puts any kind of divide between us and Him. If we truly love others, we won't do anything to hurt them, but will desire to be kind, gracious, generous, and forgiving. We will want what is best for our fellow humans. Basically, if we truly love, we won't have a reason or a desire to break any of the 10 commandments. This was the essence of Jesus' teaching while He was here on earth.

But the teachers of the Law didn't like this "new" way of thinking. The fallen angels that had been deceiving them for years were starting to lose their power over the people. They needed to gain their power back. They needed to get rid of this Jesus. They plotted and schemed. They lied and cheated. They got Jesus arrested on false charges and the people were instigated to turn on Him. They pushed and pushed until the crowded streets were filled with people shouting "Crucify Him! Crucify Him!" So, Jesus was whipped and beaten until he could no longer be recognized. His beard was pulled out by its roots, and a crown of thorns was driven into His head. He was forced to carry his own cross up a hill and was nailed to it by His hands and feet. The people He loved and cared for had turned on Him. The people he healed and fed were mocking him and killing Him. He faced the ultimate betrayal. Even His closest followers abandoned him for their own safety.

> *"Greater love has no one than this: to lay down one's life for one's friends."*
> *John 15:13*

Love is not Easily Angered/Keeps No Record of Wrong

But Jesus still loved us. Even while He was in the most agonizing pain both physically and emotionally, He still showed kindness and compassion. He gave hope to a thief, care for his mother, and forgiveness to all who had turned on him and had demanded His death. He showed the purest of Love to an undeserving world of imperfect humans who are selfish and prideful. He could have saved himself from the cross. At His word, legions of angels could have come to His rescue. But He knew this was the only way to redeem His people and restore us to fellowship with God the Father. He gave his life up to save His enemies and those who hated Him.

> *"But God demonstrates his own love for us in this: While we were still sinners, Christ died for us."*
> *Romans 5:8*

Jesus died. The earth shook. The veil in the temple that separated people from God tore in half…right down the middle. People who had died and had been laid in nearby graves came back to life. The world changed forever. His body was taken down form the cross, wrapped in cloth, and placed in a tomb someone had allowed His family to use. A huge bolder was placed in front of the door of the tomb to prevent Jesus' disciples from stealing his body and saying that He had come back to life.

Love Always Protects

But human barricades cannot stop the God of the Universe! The third day after Jesus' death dawned. Some women who followed Jesus went to the tomb to practice burial traditions on his body such as properly anointing him with oil. But they didn't know how they were going to move the stone. As they were working on this dilemma, they came upon the tomb. The boulder had been rolled away and an angel was sitting on it! The angel told them that Jesus' body was not in the tomb! He had risen from the dead! Jesus had conquered death itself to bring God's life back to us.

Love Rejoices with the Truth

Over the next several weeks, Jesus appeared to many of His followers and encouraged them. He gave specific instructions to His disciples to go out and spread the Good News of Jesus…His teachings, His death, and his resurrection. He commanded them to go and make disciples who would make more disciples, and more…until you and I were born and given the opportunity to become disciples ourselves. Disciples of love. Pure Love.

Love Always Hopes and Trusts

After Jesus had given His instructions to His followers, He left Earth again. But not to death. He ascended into Heaven to be with God the Father forever. But He did not leave us alone. The Spirit of God was sent to us to live in our hearts and teach us how to live and treat each other if we will let Him. The Holy Spirit would lead and guide us to become who God created us to be. The Holy Spirit would teach us what Pure Love is. So that we can pass that love on to others.

Jesus gave us the choice to have a new spiritual birth…a life that would grow in us much like a caterpillar in a cocoon. At the right time, we would be able to break free from this flesh and discover that we have been completely changed into something glorious. We will no longer be confined to the things of this Earth but will be able to fly to new heights in His new Kingdom...the New Heaven and the New Earth. There we will no longer be separated from God, but be restored to perfect fellowship with Him... But this time, we will understand both good and evil, and will have chosen to live forever just knowing the Goodness of God.

> *"See what great love the Father has lavished on us, that we should be called children of God! And that is what we are!"*
> *1 John 3:1a*

Think about that. Jesus, as He was dying on the cross, was thinking about you. He was making a way for you to become part of His family again. He made it possible for you to be separated from all the things of this world that drag you down and hurt you and your relationships. You can find true freedom in fellowship with the God of Creation. All you have to do is believe that this is true and accept this amazing gift from your Heavenly Father. He gave you your life to do with as you wish. But He asks you to give it back to Him and see what He can do with it. He wants to heal you from past hurts. He wants to restore you to fellowship with Him. He wants to break off the chains of anger, addiction, bitterness, depression, pride, selfishness, etc.

Love Never Fails

If you decide to give your heart and your life to Jesus and become His disciple, I PROMISE you won't regret it. You'll find out what Pure Love really means, and it will change you forever.

*"Dear friends, let us love one another, for love comes from God.
Everyone who loves has been born of God and knows God.
Whoever does not love does not know God, because God is love.
This is how God showed his love among us:
He sent his one and only Son into the world
that we might live through him.
This is love: not that we loved God, but that he loved us
and sent his Son as an atoning sacrifice for our sins.
Dear friends, since God so loved us, we
also ought to love one another."
1 John 4:7-10*

The God of all creation loves you so completely that He carefully formed you to be and look exactly like you. You are perfectly and wonderfully made. He has a specific plan for you that no one else on earth can fulfill. There is no one on earth who can impact the world the way you can. God created you with gifts, talents, and a personality that is completely unique to you. He patiently waited until exactly the right time in history to place you on this earth to be the best version of you that you could possibly be. It is up to you to learn what that means, and how to use your gifts and talents to make this world a better place and to show people what the love of God is all about.

*" For You created my inmost being;
You knit me together in my mother's womb.
I praise you because I am fearfully and wonderfully made;
Your works are wonderful, I know that full well. My frame*

was not hidden from you when I was made in the secret place,
when I was woven together in the depths of the earth.
Your eyes saw my unformed body;
All the days ordained for me were written in your
book before one of them came to be."
Psalm 139:13-16

"Now that I have a better understanding of God's love for me, how do I recognize when I've found love in people?"

The better you understand God, the more you will understand Pure Love. Read His Word for yourself, get involved in Bible Study with other believers. Get to know the God who made you. Learn how to hear His voice. Let the Holy Spirit show you how to have Pure Love yourself, then you will know what you're looking for.

Purity in Relationships

Chapter 3

"So, if I take sex out of the picture, what's left? What does a healthy relationship look like?"

My Story

I grew up fantasizing about the day I would get married, and about the man I would marry. What would he be like? What would he look like? When would we meet? How would he propose?

When I had my first "love interest" in 4th grade, I learned that not every guy was interested in staying with one girl for life. I do not consider him my "first boyfriend." I really didn't even understand what it meant to have a boyfriend at 9 years old. He would pass me "love notes," give me "gifts," and occasionally we would hold hands, but that was really all there was to that. I certainly never reciprocated any of the things he gave me. One day he passed me a note during school which read, "Will you kiss me at break?" I gave him an embarrassed smile and mumbled "no" to him on my way out the door for break time. That evening, during Wednesday night church, an older kid told me that this boy had broken up with me.

One of the reasons I do not consider him my first boyfriend was that my reaction was "ok" with a shrug. I threw away the love notes (I may have given back the gifts), and that was that. But what I took away from the experience was much more valuable than I knew at the time. Over the next few years as we got older, I watched this boy "date" girls (as long as he was interested) and then move on to the next one when he got bored. As our circle of friends matured and emotions got more and more involved, I watched my friends start to be hurt by his "games" and realized I needed to be on guard, not only for my heart, but also the hearts of my friends. I warned them about guys like him, but many of them dated anyway and inevitably got themselves hurt.

God's Gift of Purity

In addition to all the amazing things God has given you, He also gave you one of the most valuable gifts on earth. That precious gift is your purity. No, I'm not talking about your virginity. It's much deeper than that. Have you ever received a gift that was so special to you that you put it in a safe place so that it couldn't be lost or broken? Your purity is this kind of gift. This gift is yours to keep or give away. This is a much bigger responsibility than most people realize.

Purity of mind, heart, and body are given to you the moment you believe in Jesus and decide to follow Him. He gives you the Holy Spirit to guide you and to help you make the right decisions. He will teach you wrong from right and show you how to choose what is right.

Most people don't even realize that this gift is available to them! And most people don't understand its value. But I hope that by the time you're finished reading this book, you will fully grasp the beauty of the pure Love of God and how precious you are. I hope that you will learn to cherish your purity and keep it safe. But ultimately, it's up to you what you decide to do with this precious gift. You can decide to give your gift away to someone else or something else. You can keep it safe and share it with your husband when you get married. But even if you never get married, your purity is your possession to keep forever or give away. If you are careless with the gift, even if you don't give it away altogether, it can become broken or dirty.

Let's say you decide or have already decide to give your purity away to someone who is not your husband. When you and that man break up, he will have taken part of you with him. That hurts! It hurts a lot, and can be very devastating and difficult to get past. Some girls dive into depression. Some find something to numb the pain. Some move on to the next relationship quickly in order to fill the void and cover the hurt. But nothing quite satisfies, does it?

> *"If I've given my purity away, or have gotten it dirty, what can I do about it?"*

Please do not fear! There is no condemnation here. What I have for you is a promise. His promise is that He can and will restore your purity if you ask. All you need to do is humble yourself before Him, ask Him to forgive you for the things you've done wrong, and purpose to do better from this point forward. And believe me, the "better" I'm talking about here is more worth it than you can possibly imagine. The good news is you don't have to do better in your own strength! His promise is that He will be with you to help you to live a life of purity from this point forward.

Does this mean you'll never slip up or mess up? No. I mean, let's hope so, but realistically, we tend to mess up a few times before we get things right. Please don't think that if you mess up you can't come back to the Father! Even if you mess up a hundred times, He will welcome you back to Himself, clean you up, mend your heart, put you back on your feet, and give you the tools you need to do better moving forward. He is faithful and forgiving. He only wants for you to have the very best life has to offer.

"If we confess our sins, He is faithful and just and will

forgive our sins and purify us from all unrighteousness."
I John 1:9

"Though your sins are like scarlet, they shall be as white as snow; though they are red as crimson, they shall be like wool."
Isaiah 1:18

The Love of God is immeasurable and unconditional. No matter what we do in Life, there is nothing that can stop His love for us.

"For I am convinced that neither death nor life, neither angels nor demons, neither the present nor the future, nor any powers, neither height nor depth, nor anything else in all creation, will be able to separate us from the love of God that is in Christ Jesus our Lord."
Romans 8:38-39

Without the love of God in our own hearts, we cannot truly and purely love each other. Human love is faulty and conditional. We can turn from love to hate in an instant. Maybe you've even said, "that person used to be my best friend, but we never talk anymore." Something came between you. Something happened that broke trust, and that trust could not be mended.

Once God's love enters your heart, you will find that you can love others more deeply than you ever could have imagined. You will even find a certain kind of love for those who have hurt you or wronged you. Not trust or affection…love. The kind of love that can honestly hope for them to find the Love of God and allow Him to change their life.

When you truly grasp the Love of God for you, what you look for in a relationship will be drastically different from what you've been looking for so far. Your standards will rise. You will realize that God has made you worthy of receiving pure love in return, and your spirit will start to look for a spouse that understands this kind of love.

Love and purity go hand in hand. If you really love someone, you will want that love to be pure. You want to be the only person for your spouse, and you want your spouse to be the only person for you. That is a pure relationship...pure love between the two of you with nothing getting in the way.

Purity in Relationships

Now that you understand what God's pure love is, and why it's important, let's unfold what human pure love should look like and how to find it. But, in order to unravel what pure love IS, I want to start by explaining what it is NOT. Some of this may shock you.

Love is NOT:

- **TV Romance:** That's mostly infatuation, lust, or just WAY over acting.
- **Mushy gushy feelings:** While those are an important part of keeping affection alive, love has less to do with feelings than you'd expect.
- **Something you can fall out of:** Love is a choice. You don't fall in or fall out of love as if there is nothing you can do about it. That popular saying, "You can't help who you fall in love with," is an outright lie. Love is much deeper and much more powerful than that.
- Flowers, chocolates, and gifts; I mean let's face it. ANYONE can give you those things. That doesn't mean

they're willing to die for you. Or more importantly, live faithfully with you for the rest of your life through thick and thin...for better or worse...till death do you part.
- Beauty: While real love IS beautiful, it has very little to do with outward beauty or finding (or being) some one attractive or sexy. Forever kind of love won't start looking for a younger more outwardly beautiful person when you start looking old, wrinkly, saggy, and grey. If you ask your boyfriend why he's with you, and the first thing he says is "because you're hot," you may have a problem.... No, you DEFINITELY have a problem.
- Sex: Love is not sex. Sex does not mean love. Trust me on that one. Just because you give someone sex, does NOT mean that they love you. It also doesn't mean that you love them.
- Grabbing someone and kissing them in the pouring rain beneath the shelter of a gazebo, making the girl's foot "pop" and all the sparkly lights come on, and the skies clear, fireworks go off, and the moon shines down it's approval while the stars twinkle in excitement, and everyone says "Awwwwwww.": ... Again, movies.

Most of us grow up watching or reading fairy tale love stories. As we've grown, we may have graduated to Romantic Comedies and love novels which depict love found, lost, and found again. These stories always lead to that happily ever after feeling. But, they are not an accurate picture of real love. These kinds of movies really only show half ... maybe not half ... maybe a quarter of what love really is ... if that. Don't get me wrong, I'm a hopeless romantic right along with the best of them! I LOVE these stories, and I truly believe they are an important part of learning how to dream and plan for your future. Some movies can even help you learn how to recognize the guys to stay away from or help you to see the goodness in people even if they say the wrong thing at the wrong time or give the wrong first impression.

By all means Chick flick the night away. I'm right there with you.

But honestly, movies probably depict some of the unhealthiest relationship progressions I've ever seen. I mean think about it. Girl is in some sort of boring or toxic relationship. Girl bumps into boy. There's immediate attraction, but immediate distain as well. Some cute rivalry ensues, and the guy starts to realize that he really likes her. He pursues her and ultimately wins her heart...and usually her bed. The bad relationship is somehow ended possibly with some kind of duel between old flame and new prince charming and damsel is then free to move in with the new guy and they live happily ever after. These stories are cute to watch, but definitely not standards to hold in the real world.

There are many ways for a healthy relationship to develop. I want to be clear on this point. God is not in a box and would love to write your love story to be as unique as you and your future spouse. As long as you have given Him the key to your heart, and the pen to your love story, I can guarantee that you're going to be happy with the end result. I'll be revealing my own God-written love story as the book goes on.

That said, I would like to elaborate on the different stages I have noticed in the natural progression of a healthy relationship. I also discuss some of the consequences of adding sex to each stage. I can tell you from experience that being able to present your gift of purity to your spouse on your wedding night is ... priceless.

Phase 1. Friendship: Getting to know each other's likes and dislikes on a surface level. Find out if you're compatible as people. Do you like hanging around each other? Do you have fun together? Do you have common interests? Do I feel comfortable with this person? Does this person provide a safe place to talk about deep things? Is this the kind of person who can have reasonable and respectful conversations even when our opinions disagree? I think it's safe to say that most people don't think about having sex at this level.

Phase 2. Romantic Attraction: Realizing that you might be looking at a long-term relationship. This part is the mushy gushy level. It's exciting and sweet while you're trying to impress each other and learning how to express your feelings on a romantic level. Adding sex at this level makes breaking up more painful if you find out that you are not compatible romantically.

Phase 3. Settling Into the Relationship: This is the time when you seriously start looking at you're relationship long-term. This is the point at which you should start thinking about and talking about whether or not you are both pursuing marriage. If one or both of you are not, you should end the relationship before someone gets hurt.

Now is the time to start asking some questions. Are you on the same page spiritually? Do you both have the same life goals? Can you handle each other's annoying habits? Do you have each other's back in any situation?

Phase 4. Getting Serious: As a couple, once you have decided that marriage is the goal, it's time to dig deep into the relationship to weed out the potential "deal breakers." Are you both pursuing God with the same intensity? Do your morals and beliefs line up with each other's? Are you willing to put aside the idea of never dating anyone else? Are you both willing to take your future wherever God leads? Do you get along with each other's families, or at least can differences be set aside for the sake of the relationship? Do you both want children, and if so how many? Are there cultural differences that need to be worked through? Or are there strong family traditions that clash with each other? All of these things should be talked through at this stage of your relationship so that you can still break it off if there are differences that one or both of you are unable to or unwilling to compromise on.

During this time, if you haven't already, you should start experiencing conflict in your relationship. This is normal and healthy. You should start learning how to work through conflict. You need to learn to be respectful to each other and to be able to come to an agreement or an understanding in each situation. If your arguments become more intense over time, if you're having them more often, or if you're having trouble resolving them, you need to seriously consider the possibility of ending the relationship. Every healthy relationship will have arguments, but the arguments should become shorter and further apart over time as you learn how to resolve them together.

Adding sex to this mixture throws it off balance. Either sex becomes the way to resolve conflict, covers up the issue, or draws attention away from the issue so it is never resolved - in some cases, sex can actually make the intensity of the conflict worse if the couple has not learned how to resolve things in a healthy way. Many people end up feeling trapped at this point. They've realized that they are not compatible with this person, or that the other person isn't invested in the relationship long-term, but they have already invested so much of their time, body, life, finances, and even their home and now they don't know how to get out of the relationship or live without the other person.

Phase 5. Engagement: This is the time of the relationship where you have decided that you can handle life together and you are starting to build and combine your lives. This can be a very fun, but also stressful time as the couple begins planning out the details of their wedding, where they are going to live, and what their future will hold together as a family.

Adding sex to the mix here is like giving a student alcohol and giving them a buzz (or straight up drunk) right before a test. They may or may not pass the test, but even if they do manage to pass, their score won't be as high because their judgment will be clouded. The time of engagement is like cramming for finals in your senior year. You're literally laying down a foundation for the rest of your life. You want to be clear headed in order for that foundation to be level and solid.

Many people decide to start having sex once they have decided to get married. "No big deal. We're getting married anyway." All the time and effort put into the relationship has bonded you. You're invested. But now that you've started having sex, one or both of you start to lose the traction you've gained toward building a strong marriage. Sometimes, having sex before marriage literally breaks up a couple. For others, it brings a sense of complacency. You've started having sex, so why not go ahead and move in together? The excitement and anticipation of planning your wedding starts to fade. You've already combined your bodies and then your homes. You've settled into your life and now you're too busy and broke to plan a wedding, so you put it off… and put it off… and the wedding never happens. For one of you, it's like, "Were already living together and I'm getting all of my sexual needs met, so why bother getting married?" For the other person it's, "Why can't we make the commitment? Is our relationship not that important?"

It's like running a race together. You see the finish line coming. You look at each other, high five, and walk off the track before you actually win the race. What a letdown.

Phase 6. Marriage: Notice, I didn't say "wedding." The wedding is just one day of your entire life. I hope your wedding day is magical. I hope it's everything you ever wanted. I hope everyone you love is there to celebrate with you. I hope you have an excellent photographer. It's a day to celebrate! You've gone through a bunch of things together, and you still want to spend the rest of your lives together. Have fun, have all the traditions you love, and may it be a day to remember. But, it's just the beginning of your story.

After the wedding, you have to go home with that person. Learning how to live together with someone is hard. If you have not learned the lessons you needed to learn in the early stages of your relationship, you'll have to learn them all at once…right now. Like starting your first year of college and asking to take all of the classes for all four years in your first year. The stress of trying to learn it all in one shot could break you. Doing the same with relationships has led to way too many broken hearts and has ended way too many marriages, and families.

There's a reason they say the first year of marriage is the hardest. But, it doesn't have to be so hard that it breaks you. I am not saying a couple can't survive through any situation. But, God's plan minimizes the risk of pain, heartache, break up, and divorce. God's plan allows a couple to work through it a little at a time. He helps you to master each lesson and pass each test before going on to the next.

Marriage is every day after your wedding. All the ups and downs. All the good times and bad. All the fun and disappointment. The dreams that come true and the tragedies that befall us. Day in and day out living with your best friend and making life work together. Paying the bills, keeping food on the table, maybe raising a family, and even a few pets. I hope you get to travel the world together. But if you don't, I hope that every day, no matter how good or bad, you will have no regrets about the decision you made on who you are going to spend the rest of your life with.

Adding sex to marriage is like adding whipped cream and chocolate syrup on top of a huge bowl of your favorite ice cream.

It's your reward for all the hard work you put into making sure you've got the best chance at a lifelong marriage. You and your spouse have built your house together. It's on a solid foundation, the color is just right, it's got all the right rooms in all the right places. You received your keys at your wedding. Now, it's time to move the furniture in and decorate. It's the fun part. Enjoy it!

> *"All of this sounds so great! How do I get it in my own life? How do I find my own Prince Charming?"*

Patience and trust in God's plan for your life. Sounds boring, I know. But I promise it's the best way to find real love. Until then, let's get you some great information on what Pure Love really is so that you recognize it when you see it.

Love is Patient

Chapter 4

Adjective: "able to accept or tolerate delays, problems, or suffering without becoming annoyed or anxious."

My Story

I started hoping for and dreaming about my future husband started when I was 12 years old. I had a dream about him around this time. I was walking down a street walking towards my wedding. I looked down and realized I was wearing my wedding dress. It was gently flared around my ankles and had white vines with small flowers coming up the front. I came across a big building with glass walls. The glass was tinted so I had to walk close to it to see inside. There were children playing inside. I looked up and saw a reflection of a man behind me. I realized I was late for my wedding, and it must be my future husband behind me.

I turned around to face him. He was taller than me, had dark hair, and was holding a box. At first, I thought it was a ring box and my heart sank. I thought he was returning my ring and breaking off our wedding. Then, he turned the box, and I could see that it was a bracelet box. A gift. I was so happy! I looked up at him. He said, "I thought about it, and I realized that I could never stop loving you." Then I woke up. This dream birthed hope in me that the man I would marry would be strong and kind. He would be forgiving of my flaws, and we would be happy together.

Shortly after I had the dream, I decided to design my wedding dress on paper. My goal was to have the dress made for my wedding. My mom bought me a hope chest and taught me how to put some hopes and dreams about my wedding into the box. Just for fun, we went to bridal shows where I collected ideas and samples to put into my hope chest. One of our favorite games was to go to jewelry stores and look at wedding sets. We would give the jeweler the impression that I was planning to get married soon and would ambiguously answer questions as to my future husband's identity. "

> *"I'm not sure where he is right now."*
> *"He could be working."*
> *"We haven't set a date yet."*

Around that time, I finally had the opportunity to go through the class my mom had created. By this time she had changed the name to "Keypers," and her main theme was "Being a Keyper and finding one." The lessons you have learned in this book have their foundation in the curriculum she created, and the valuable lessons I have learned from my own experience and from the experiences of those around me.

Living a pure life and saving my virginity for the man I would marry was always something very special to me. It was a badge I proudly wore on my spirit. I really never understood why this incredible gift from God was something that people didn't save for marriage. I watched my mom council hurt, scared, and lonely girls, many of which were my friends. I saw the pain and heartache that came with breaking up with someone you thought you were going to be with forever. I saw the fear and uncertainty that came along with suddenly discovering you're going to be a mom and you haven't even finished high school yet.

I began to realize that saving sex for marriage wasn't just a rule God or our parents placed on us to control our lives. Saving sex for marriage was much more than an incredible gift I could give to my future husband. It was also a way to protect myself, my heart, and my body from all the pain associated with breakups, Sexually Transmitted Diseases (STDs), abuse, and unplanned pregnancies. I also realized that it was something that I was also doing for my future husband…a beautiful gift I would offer to him on our wedding night. That was when I decided that not only would I save my virginity as a wedding present for my husband I would also save our first kiss for our wedding day. I also decided to trust God so completely with my love life that I would not date until I met the man I was going to marry. I wanted to be so sure about God's direction that my first boyfriend would eventually be my husband. I decided to patiently wait for God to write my love story.

The Patience of God

To explain how patient God is, I need to refer to the Old Testament in the Bible. God's special people were the Israelites. He chose them to create a great nation that would eventually bring about the Messiah (Jesus) who would save the world from their sins. You would think that being God's chosen people, they would have always honored Him, always obeyed Him, and always did the right thing. But they were a stubborn people (much like us). Time and time again, they would complain, disobey, or even start worshiping idols made of stone, wood, metal, or whatever else they came up with naming as a deity.

You would think that God would be so mad that He would say "Forget it! You're not my chosen people anymore! I'll go find someone else!" Actually, He almost did that a few times. But, He kept to His Word and his promise to Abraham. The people would turn from their evil and back to Him, and He forgave them … over and over again … for thousands of years. In fact, He is still forgiving and being patient with us to this day. Why? Because of Hi great LOVE for us. Definitely not because we deserve it …

because we don't.

"Being Patient is Hard!"

We live in a world where everything is available at the click of a button, the opening of a door, or the ring of a phone. Waiting is simply not "in style." But there is an old saying, "anything worth having is worth waiting for." Sure, you can get a relationship started up pretty quickly. You're adorable, beautiful, smart, witty, who wouldn't want you? And you really want to be loved, feel accepted, captivating, and important to someone. We're created with these desires! It's totally normal!

I'm sure you felt the "but" coming … What most people really don't get is that no human will ever actually be able to fulfill those desires in you. Sure, they can momentarily make you feel good about yourself and your relationships. But God is the only One who can really fulfill those needs in you. When He does, and you're a complete person, THEN you're ready to have the icing on the cake … the husband who will show you the earthly form of God's kind of love.

It can feel discouraging to wait for the right match. Maybe because you see others around you who look happy in their relationships, and you feel that you should have that kind of happiness too. Maybe because your standards are high, and it's taking forever to find one that will meet them. Maybe because all the good guys around you are already taken, and you feel that the right match doesn't exist!

If the desire to find the right husband remains in your heart, be patient! God is preparing him for you just as much as He is preparing you for him. Are you willing to wait as long as it takes? What if the right guy never comes? What if he comes, but you somehow miss the signs? … Do you trust God to lead you? Will you be obedient to Him and keep your purity safe in your care forever? Or will you give it away for the sake of desire?

> *"Let's say I'm starting to buy this whole purity thing ... how do I handle waiting?"*

If you've decided that waiting for the right man to come along is worth the wait, trust me, you've made the right decision. But if you're not wrapping yourself up in relationships like most of society is doing, it's easy to feel a little lost ... or bored. So, what should you do in the meantime?

Being Patient for the Right Relationship

Live - Watch - Pray

Live your life. Make plans with friends. Work and make money so you can do exciting and new things. Plan an adventure. Get to know people. Make new friends. Volunteer at a non-profit. Once you move out of your parent's house, take at least a year to live by yourself and support yourself. Build on your resume. Make a career plan and go for it! Become self-sufficient so that you will never find yourself caught up in a relationship that you feel you can't get out of because you don't know how to be on your own.

Watch how other people handle relationships. Start taking notes (either in your head or in your journal) on what works and what doesn't. See how other couples handle conflict. Learn to recognize "red flags" in relationships. You might even be able to save some friends from bad relationships if you notice something just isn't right.

Pray for your future husband. Pray for your future children. Pray for yourself. Connect with God. Build a relationship with Jesus. Ground your spirit and your emotions in the One who loves you unconditionally, completely, purely, and more than life itself. Find yourself in the eyes of The One who created you. Work on becoming the person He designed you to be. When you are that close with Jesus, no relationship good or bad can shake your confidence in who you are.

> *"Yes but, while I'm doing all that, how do I find My Prince Charming?"*

While you're living, watching, and praying, you will begin to learn how to differentiate "Prince Charming" from "Prince Not-so-Charming," so that you don't get yourself caught in a bad relationship. Let's go over a few examples of "Prince Not," so you'll have an idea of what to look for.

"Prince Vain" is full of himself. He's the guy who is cute and knows it. He appears self-confident, which can be a really good quality, but if you watch him closely, he's a little too self-focused. He's the kind of guy who needs you to stroke his ego. He'll want to hear from you how wonderful he is. And if you don't say it enough, he will.

A man like this typically doesn't know how to admit when he is wrong. It's too embarrassing to admit his faults, which is why he builds himself up with his accomplishments. He rarely truly thinks about others unless there is something he can get out of it.

He'll flatter you and make you feel special, but only because he's looking to get something from you. When he realizes that you really are serious about waiting to have sex until you're married, "Prince Vain" will either push you to give in, get frustrated and angry, or turn and run to the next girl.

"Pride goes before destruction, A haughty spirit before a fall."
Proverbs 16:18

"Prince Vain" is NOT worthy of you or your purity.

Watch out for "Prince Romance!" He is really good at putting on a show. He can plan the perfect date that will pull all your guards down. When he realizes that you're serious about waiting to have sex until you're married, he's the type that may be hurt or make you feel guilty because of all the effort he put into romancing you, or he may tell you that he really respects you and agrees with you … for a while. Then when he feels that he has your guards down enough, he'll try again with all that sweet talking and puppy dog eyes. This is because deep down he really doesn't respect you or your wishes. All he really wants is excitement in your relationship…and sex.

"Prince Romance" is too focused on feelings. He is easily hurt or may be the jealous type. As soon as your relationship gets boring, or you start to argue, he'll start saying things like "…maybe we shouldn't be together, then." He may also start accusing you of cheating on him or may start cheating on you. Or both. It's all part of a weird high he gets from keeping the relationship "exciting."

PLEASE REMEMBER THIS: If you start to see these red flags in your relationship, it is NOT because you are actually boring or argumentative. Trying to make yourself more exciting, sexier, or less argumentative will NOT make him stay. It may hold off his leaving for a little while, but he will eventually get bored and leave because that's who HE is, and it's NOT about you. To him, you are simply another chapter in his life, not a real partner in life.

"Charm is deceptive, and beauty is fleeting;
But a woman who fears the Lord is to be praised."

Proverbs 31:30

"Prince Romance" is NOT worthy of you or your purity.

"Prince Treasure" is only interested in things. He's the type of guy who likes to buy things for himself. He'll spend money on you if he thinks it'll make you happy. He believes that he can "buy" your love. When your relationship gets serious enough that you are starting to argue, he'll generally think that a bouquet of flowers or box of chocolates will fix the issue. He doesn't realize that issues actually need to be worked out. He's also the type of prince who may throw what he's spent on you back in your face when things aren't working out.

When you are married or living together, he might start talking about "my money" verses "your money." If he earns the majority of the income, he is likely to use that fact to get what he wants or keep you from getting what you want.

"Prince Treasure" is not so interested in keeping your purity safe. He's more interested in getting it for himself. You and your purity are more of a possession to him than anything. Once he gets it, he will probably get bored with it. He'll start looking elsewhere for the next woman to "conquer." He may be the kind of high school kid who actually has a goal of sleeping with every cute girl on campus ... or at least every cute virgin. Very superficial.

When he realizes you're serious about not having sex until you're married, he will be "so over" your relationship.

*"For where your treasure is,
there your heart will be also."*

Matthew 6:21

"Prince Treasure" is NOT worthy of you or your purity.

"Prince Jealous" is the kind of guy who will want you to spend all your time with him. It's cute at first. It will feel as though his world revolves around you. "He's so sweet, he ALWAYS wants us to be together. It's kind of cute how he pouts when I tell him that I'm going to go hang out with my friends. He just needs to be around me. I'll go ahead and tell my friends I can't go this time…" "It's nice that he's taking an interest in what I wear. I guess it won't hurt anything to just wear what he wants me to wear." "It's so cute how he's jealous when other guys talk to me. He's just looking out for me." Ladies, these are HUGE warning signs.

At first, his jealousy may even make you feel safe. But, over time, if you're paying attention, you'll begin to notice that you really don't see much of your own friends anymore. You spend all of your time with him and avoid talking with other guys even when there's nothing going on between you and them. You'll start dressing yourself according to what you know he will want you to wear and avoid certain outfits that you really like just, because he will disapprove.

"Prince Jealous" is a very dangerous guy. He's the kind of guy that has a very real potential to turn into an abuser. Physical and emotional abusers will typically start out as the jealous type. When he realizes you're serious about waiting to have sex until marriage, he may become angry and try to force you to do things you do not want to do. He may use guilt and/or fear to coerce you into giving up your values. You may be in a position where you do not feel safe saying "no." So, when you begin to recognize "Prince Jealous," avoid alone time with him, and get out of the relationship as quickly as you can.

> *"A heart at peace gives life to the body,*
> *but envy rots the bones."*
> *Proverbs 14:30*

"Prince Jealous" is NOT worthy of you or your purity.

These are just a few examples of "Prince Nots" you are sure to run across in your life. Have you met "Prince Jerk," "Prince Disrespectful," "Prince Poor Me," "Prince Too Cool," or "Prince Do This for me?" All of these princes will display good qualities at one point or another, but if they're living up to any of these names on a more regular basis, put up your guard. Chances are they are not your "Prince Charming."

Now that you have some idea of what to avoid, let's learn how to recognize "Prince Charming" so that you will find a Godly man to marry when the time is right.

As you look for good qualities in men, it is really important that you keep your guards up around your heart. It is far too easy to find good qualities in men and develop unhealthy crushes. Remember, this might be a "Prince Charming," but it may not be YOUR "Prince Charming." Allow God to work on you and when you're ready, He will bring a good match to you at the right time… someone who has allowed God to work on him as well. He will be patient with you as he will understand the importance of keeping your purity safe.

Look around at some godly men in your life or at least some strong authority figures that you see as grounded and good men. Note some of their good qualities … things you admire. Here are some examples of "Prince Charming."

"Prince Reliable" is hard working. He's the kind of prince with goals and ambitions. He knows the importance of being to work on time and doing a good job. He'll be promoted and successful at whatever he puts his mind to. He's the kind of prince who will make your relationship a top priority. He likes to succeed, so he will be dedicated to making your relationship succeed. When there is a problem in your relationship, he will want to work to fix it. Keeping things broken between you is unacceptable because it will mean that your relationship is not the best it can be.

> *"All hard work brings a profit,*
> *but mere talk leads only to poverty."*
> *Proverbs 14:23*

"Prince Authentic" is real. What you see is what you get. You won't have to worry about him hiding anything, because he's not the type. While this may make it difficult for him to plan a surprise party, it will give you the assurance that he is not hiding a part of his personality or his past from you that you won't like.

The only way you can be sure you're recognizing "Prince Authentic" is by watching him over time. Most people cannot fake a personality for more than a year.

> *"Many claim to have unfailing love,*
> *but a faithful person who can find?"*
> *Proverbs 20:6*

"Prince Sincere" is honest. Lying of any kind is never a good quality for any person to possess. He understands how detrimental this can be to your relationship. Rest assured that he will be honest with you about his feelings, and truly want to work out any issues in your relationship. If "Prince Sincere" wants to make your relationship work, he will sincerely want to do what is right for both of you. Your relationship will be important to him.

Please don't lie in any relationship. It's very unhealthy. But be especially honest with Prince Sincere. If you are not, it will hurt him deeply that you don't trust him enough to be open and honest with him.

> "The honor of good people will lead them,
> but those who hurt others will be destroyed
> by their own false ways."
> Proverbs 11:3

"Prince Compassion" is kind. Do you know anyone who opens doors for people, or is the first to make sure someone is ok when they've fallen? He might be "Prince Compassion." He's the kind of guy who is good with kids, helps the teacher, and respects his parents. He will be in tune to your feelings (most of the time) and want to keep peace in your home. Your happiness will be a top priority to him.

Just be careful that you do not take "Prince Compassion" for granted. He is kind and generous while putting others first but may not let you know if he's hurting or if you've offended him. He also may find it hard for others to do things for him, or to show compassion toward him when he's down.

> "A gentle answer turns away wrath,

but a harsh word stirs up anger."
Proverbs 15:1

Your "Prince Charming" will probably exhibit some mixture of qualities of several of these princes. He might be romantic and hard working. He might be honest and compassionate. But he is still human. He may also have some of the not so good qualities of the first princes. He will have both good and bad qualities. But, "Mr. Wrong" will have more of the negative qualities, and less of the positive qualities. "Mr. Right" will have more of the positive qualities and less of the negative ones… and he will be working on getting those under control.

Please trust me, ladies. "Prince Charming" is so worth the wait. Be patient, God is preparing him for you just as much as He is preparing you for him. Even if you never get married, God will always love you and there is no greater love than God's love.

"But God demonstrated his own love for us in this:
While we were still sinners, Christ died for us."
Romans 5:8

" For I am convinced that neither death nor life,
neither angels nor demons, neither the present nor the
future, nor any powers, neither height nor depth,
nor anything else in all creation, will be able to separate us
from the love of God that is in Christ Jesus our Lord."
Romans 8:38-39

Love is Kind

Chapter 5

Noun: "the quality of being friendly, generous, and considerate."

My Story

During high school, everyone knew I didn't date. I'm sure there were snickers behind my back as there were a few to my face. I didn't mind, though. A senior girl who was graduating lovingly left to me a poster with pictures plastered all over it of "cute guys" on one side and "not cute" guys on the other side, because, apparently, I didn't know how to tell the difference. The truth is, I just wasn't interested in guys… not that I didn't have a high school crush, but I knew I would never date my crush because he wasn't the kind of person I could see myself marrying.

Yet, as I drew closer to God and talked with Him about my many feelings, I felt Him put an idea on my heart. I felt that he was telling me that my future husband would not be a virgin. I was going to be someone's "second chance." As much as I cherished purity and my virginity, I surprised myself by being ok with the idea of giving myself to someone who didn't save himself for marriage. I trusted God with my whole life and knew He would not let me down in this area. As long as this man met my top three requirements (love God, love our family, love ministry), God could give me whoever He wanted to.

Recognizing God's Kindness

Did you know that God is kind? Have you ever thought about it? His entire creation was built with us in mind. It was perfect before we messed it up. And even then, when Adam and Eve sinned, He immediately set a plan in motion to fix the problem and bring us back to Him.

He sent His Son, Jesus, to take the fall for everything we have ever done wrong. We should all be dead for our wrongs, but He died so that we don't have to. He suffered the most horrific death in all of history so that we have the option of spending eternity with Him.

His kindness doesn't stop there! He also gave us free will. We get to make the decision for ourselves if we want to be thankful for what He did for us. It's our choice to get to know Him or not. He refuses to force His love on us or command us to be grateful. He took on the punishment for our wrongs, and the most horrific death KNOWING that many of us wouldn't accept His precious gift of eternal life. THAT is undeserved kindness.

God took great care when He made you. He knew that you would play a vitally important role in this world, so He carefully planned out every part of your being to be perfect for your part in history. He picked out your hair color and type, your skin tone, your eye color, your shape, and your height. He designed your personality, your gifts, your voice, and your skills.

> *"My bones were not hidden from You when I was made in secret and put together with care in the deep part of the earth."*
> *Psalm 139:15*

He picked out a family for you and placed you in their lives to put you exactly where you needed to be to make the most impact for this world. Even if your childhood circumstances make you wonder what on earth He was thinking, please understand that He still had a plan. Even though the humans around you may have made the wrong or even horrific choices, He knew it all and has carefully orchestrated a plan to use it all for your good and His glory…if you let Him.

> *"I praise You because I am fearfully and wonderfully made; Your works are wonderful, I know that full well."*
> *Psalm 139:14*

God created a perfect plan for your life before your parents even thought of you. He knew what He was doing when He gave you your unique gifts and talents. Your voice and your skills were specifically picked out for your personality so that you would be able to bring His love to those that only you can touch in your own unique way.

> *"Before I formed you in the womb*
> *I knew you.*
> *Before you were born*
> *I set you apart;*
> *I appointed you as a prophet to the nations."*
> *Jeremiah 1:5*

Don't you think that a God who would do all of that would be faithful to meet your every need? Remember this, though. You might be praying for something that you THINK you need, while He is preparing for you what He KNOWS you need. So, if you feel your prayers aren't being answered, be patient. He will show you exactly what you need when the time is right.

> *"…for your Father knows what you need*

> *before you ask Him."*
> *Matthew 6:8*

> *"And my God will meet all your needs according to the riches of His glory in Christ Jesus."*
> *Philippians 4:19*

If God knew you before you were even born, has a plan for your life, knows what you need before you even ask Him, and promises to supply all of your needs, don't you think that He is capable, willing, and even desires to give you a husband who will enhance your life and your walk with Him?

Let's Talk About Pure Friendships

Think about some of your friends you would consider "kind." When we say someone is kind, we usually mean that they are friendly, look out for others, and like to help people. They think about others before themselves. They lift you up when you're down.

Hmm...so, the characteristics you're looking for in a husband sound a lot like characteristics you might look for in a friend! There's a good reason for this. Relationships tend to be stronger when they start out as friendships. So, if you really want to find the right man for you, I encourage you to hold off on dating until you're ready for marriage. That way, you'll develop strong friendships with guys and get to know what they're really like before you start thinking about them romantically. You'll also learn to recognize the characteristics you're looking for in a husband without clouding your judgment with infatuation. You'll avoid a LOT of heartbreak if you decide to do it this way.

"How do I be 'just friends' with a guy without it getting weird?"

Society makes that difficult, doesn't it? Whenever you hang out with a guy, someone is bound to assume you like each other. Been there, done that.

I had a guy friend in college. I considered him a brother. We related on an intellectual level and actually got very close. So close, in fact, that most of my friends thought I liked him romantically, and our pastor suggested that we spend less alone time with each other so as to not give the wrong impression to each other or to others. It was difficult for me to do that, as I felt that among my friends he "got me" the most. Now that I'm older, I understand the wisdom in our pastor's advice.

Unfortunately, people labeling or misunderstanding you is just something you'll have to live with. As long as you and your friends know where you stand, you should be fine. One way for you to set yourself up for success is to understand what relationships look like at different levels. This way, you'll know what to expect, what to watch for, and how to act so that you don't lead anyone on. We're talking about kindness, right? Well, kindness in this case is everyone knowing where they stand so that no one gets hurt.

We've already evaluated what a healthy relationship progression is, but now let's take a deeper look at each stage of a relationship and what boundaries should look like during each stage.

Friendship

Friendship is hanging out together, but not romantically. Going to the movies with friends, getting a bite to eat with friends, hanging out at someone's house with others present, these are examples of fairly "safe" things you can do with guys to get to know each other without feelings getting in the way.

During this time in your life, you should be praying for God to reveal to you the person He has planned to be your future husband. You should be praying for God to strengthen him and make him into the man of God that you can respect and submit to. You should be praying that God will make you into the woman of God your future husband will be honored to have as his wife.

Dating

Dating is hanging out together with the understanding that you both like each other. This can be in groups, or not, but you should never be completely alone. The point is to see if your feelings for each other can lead to courtship, engagement, and marriage. At this point in your relationship, it is vitally important that you take time to talk about personal boundaries.

When you set boundaries with the guy you're planning on dating, you get the opportunity to see how kind he really is. If he truly respects you, he will honor your boundaries, and should have some boundaries of his own which you will need to respect.

It is very important for you to decide what your boundaries are BEFORE you get into a relationship. If you wait until you start a relationship to decide what you will and will not do physically, you are likely to cross some lines you are not comfortable with before you even realize that you are not comfortable with crossing them.

If the guy you are considering dating is not ok with your boundaries, he's not worth your time. Even if he hesitates but agrees, he may push those boundaries later, leaving you in a very uncomfortable position and probably a nasty breakup. Most teen and young adult guys won't continue dating someone once they realize that the boundaries are firm, so you need to be VERY clear that you're not going to budge on your boundaries BEFORE you put your heart (and his) on the line.

Recommended boundaries for dating:

- Never be completely alone. Always have people nearby. Parents, friends, another couple, or crowds in public places.
- Holding hands is ok as long as you're comfortable
- Short hugs are ok as long as you're comfortable
- Kisses on hand, cheek, or forehead are ok as long as you're comfortable
- Sitting close to each other with or without arms around each other should be evaluated. If it becomes too much for one of you, you should back off.
- While dating, I do not recommend kisses on the mouth or anywhere more "personal" or "sensual" (such as the neck or shoulder) It awakens feelings that are very difficult to put back to sleep.
- Touching private areas including butt is not ok
- Hands under clothing is not ok

In addition to praying that God will make you both into men and women of God, Pray together and separately for God to reveal to each of you if your relationship is within His plan for your life. Even if you are both going after God, He may have a different future planned out for each of you. It would be very difficult to have a happy marriage if he was called to be a missionary to Germany, and you were called to be an architect in ancient Egypt. Or, if he's called to work with NASA, and you're called to be a schoolteacher in Northern Main... You get the idea.

Courtship

Courtship does not look very different from dating on the

outside. The difference is in your emotional investment to the relationship. Basically, it's the step of your relationship where things have gotten serious. You've gotten to know each other better and the excitement of a new relationship has worn down just a little. By now, you should be starting to deal with a few relationship and personality issues. At this point, as a couple, you need to decide if your relationship is heading toward marriage, or if you really can't see spending the rest of your life together. If it's the latter, you really need to put a stop to the relationship before either of you get more hurt or waste any more of each other's time.

When it comes to boundaries, you should have another discussion. You've gotten to know each other better. At this point, you should feel safe with each other, and you should know that you are going to continue to respect each other's boundaries.

Recommended boundaries for courtship.
- Almost everything you've decided on during dating should still stand.
- Kisses on the mouth may now be ok. But maybe not. You both need to decide if you're ready for that. And if you decide that you are, and try it, but it stirs up too much in either of you, you should pull back.
- Cuddling should be ok as long as it's understood that if it becomes difficult for one of you, you will back off.
- Touching private areas is still off limits
- Hands under clothing is still a very bad idea
- French kissing is not advisable. It's a far more sexual and intimate act, and I personally recommend saving it for marriage, but at least for engagement.
- You may decide that you can start spending some time alone, but you need to be aware that the sexual tension is going to be stronger. You need to limit your time alone and understand that if the tension becomes diffi

cult for one of you, you need to immediately separate. This is for your emotional safety. If something does happen and you end up not getting married, you'll be happy that you did not cross any lines.
- Agree to some kind of "escape plan" if one of you is becoming a little too "excited." It could be a code word or phrase…it might help to have something silly to keep things light. "If you work as a security guard in a Samsung store, does that make you a Guardian of the Galaxy?" Or "If Cinderella's shoe fit perfectly, why did it fall off?"
- Sexual tension is particularly stronger at night. Be aware of this when you're setting boundaries. You may decide that being alone during the day is ok, but at night is just not wise.

During courtship, I highly advise that you and your possible future husband establish a regular time to pray together and do devotions together. Getting into a habit of focusing on God together will build a strong foundation for your marriage. This is the kind of foundation that will help your marriage to last. Separately, you should each continue to pray for each other.

Engagement

Engagement is the point in your relationship where you've gotten through a few major arguments, seen each other's good side and bad side, and have decided for sure that you definitely want to spend the rest of your lives together. Maybe, your man will have sought the approval of your loved ones and have planned and executed some romantic proposal. Maybe you're wedding dress shopping, planning decorations, picking out bridesmaids and groomsmen, figuring out who you're going to invite, and deciding what kinds of memories you want to take away from your special day. But, of course, every relationship is different. Hopefully, your wedding is as unique and wonderful as your relationship.

When it comes to boundaries, there should be very little difference between engagement and courtship. At this point in your relationship, everything gets crazy while you're preparing for your wedding, and preparing to spend the rest of your lives together. The LAST thing you need is the added complication of sex and/or more sexual tension. Guard yourselves so that you can get through and make it to your wedding day without going completely insane.

I do not particularly recommend long engagements. If you've been together for over a year (and this is after having known each other as friends beforehand), done all of your homework, gotten through some relationship issues, still like each other, and are 100% sure this marriage is planned out by God, 6 months to a year is a good window for engagement. 3 months is doable if you're a simple wedding planner (seriously, only after you've done all the work to make sure this is the right move for your future). I don't necessarily recommend shorter engagements, as it takes a little time to let it sink in that you are going to be living with this other human being for the rest of your life. Engagements longer than a year are extremely difficult. Been there, done that. The sexual tension becomes more intense the closer you get to your wedding. Once you've decided that this is the man for you, you should set a date and focus on planning.

Consistent connection to each other and to God is vitally important when you're planning on spending the rest of your life together. Ask others to pray for your relationship. Get pre-marriage counseling to work out some of the kinks. You'll want to work out as many issues as humanly possible BEFORE you're with each other 24/7. There will be PLENTY of other issues to deal with while learning to live together. Trust me.

I know this is a lot to take in right now, but I want you to have a good grasp on why relationships are designed to progress this way. If you work out the issues a little at a time, it allows for a much easier "out" at just about any stage from dating to engagement, in case you decide it's not going to work out. I've seen it too many times. Couples jump right into a relationship without getting to know each other or jump right into bed before finding out things about each other that are incredibly important. ... Like do you want kids and how many, or where do you see your career going? What are your religious beliefs? How do you feel about drinking, smoking, drugs, political views, or world issues?

Sex out of order complicates relationships, or completely distracts from these important line items. When you take things slower, you have the opportunity to work your issues out a little at a time instead of all at once. Believe me; you do not want to deal with them all at once. It has destroyed marriages ... from newlyweds right up to couples who have been married for 35 years!

Kindness is doing everything in the right order. It's kindness towards yourself and kindness towards your future husband.

Love Does Not Envy

Chapter 6

Noun: 'a feeling of discontented or resentful longing aroused by someone else's possessions, qualities, or luck. Example: 'Everyone has a boyfriend but me. It's not fair!'

Verb: desire to have a quality, possession, or other desirable attribute belonging to (someone else). Example: 'I want her boyfriend, so I want to steal him from her!'

My Story

Then came high school graduation and the excitement of moving away from home for college. I just KNEW I would find my future husband during college. I was "out in the world" and learning how to make it on my own. Even though I did end up with a college crush, nothing ever came of it, and my friends started believing that I would never get married. In their opinion, my standards were too high. I was asked "How is any guy going to know that you're available if you keep that ring on your finger?" My answer came surprisingly easily. "If the guy doesn't know me well enough to know what this ring means, he is not worth my time." I wanted the best God had for me. I didn't want to settle for just anyone. So, casual dating wasn't even on my radar. The plan was simple. I would live my life and get to know people. As I made friends, my future husband would show up. We would get to know each other, and eventually our friendship would grow into something more."

Was I envious of my friends who were getting engaged or married? Honestly, I knew I was young and still had time. I enjoyed being with my friends and rejoiced with them when they found someone to marry. I was too busy with my own life to worry about wanting someone else's life.

The Jealousy of God

> *"I am the Lord; that is My Name; my glory I give to no other, nor my praise to carved idols."*
> *Isaiah 42:8*

Think about this: God created humans to have fellowship with Him. He gave us the earth to rule over and populate. But we, as humans, rejected the one rule He had…not to eat from the tree of the knowledge of good and evil. Eventually, we rejected His existence altogether and created statues out of rock, wood, or metal, and worshipped our own creations instead of The Creator. This made God jealous…for all the right reasons. He gave us EVERYTHING and we thanked rock, wood, and stone instead of thanking HIM.

Now, I'm pretty sure that you don't bow down to rock, wood, or stone idols, but do you have other things that are more important to you than God? How about social media? Entertainment? Acceptance from your peers? These can be difficult questions to ask ourselves, but it's important to recognize things in our lives that we may be putting before God. It may be time to rearrange our priorities.

Envy in Relationships

Envy and pride will put strain on any relationship. Envy has to do with the attitude behind the want. It's perfectly fine to want something. It's great to work hard to be able to attain the same thing as someone else, but if your attitude stinks, and you feel negatively toward another person for having something you want, or if you feel a compulsion to take what belongs to that person, you've got a real problem and need an attitude adjustment.

I have heard so many songs ... popular songs ... of people wailing and complaining because someone else has the man they want or begging someone not to take their man away or they are simply going to die, or conniving to steal someone else's man, or wanting to kill their significant other because they were caught cheating. I've got to say it ... it's PATHETIC! Good grief girl, wake up! You're worth more than that! If that guy is easily swayed by another pretty face (or butt), that dude is not worth your time! Walk away. Or let him walk away. You're worth waiting for! You're worth pursuing! You're worth cherishing. You're worth being the ONE and ONLY woman in a man's life. And what does it say about the kind of girl who wants to take someone else's man away? How would YOU feel if someone was flirting with your man trying to take him away from you? Whatever happened to "Us girls have to stick together?" Don't do to someone else what you wouldn't want done to you. I don't care if it HAS happened to you. Don't do it to someone else. It NEVER ends well. Never.

Ok, rant over.

"If I'm not supposed to envy what others have, does that mean that I'm not supposed to want or need anything?"

Not at all what I'm saying! God created us with needs. But we tend to look at our wants and turn them into needs. How many times have you said, "I really need some chocolate right now!" Do you really need it, or do you just really want it? Ok...you might actually need it if you're PMSing.

So, how do we separate our wants from our needs? Let's start by identifying our needs. God has created us with three categories of needs. They are emotional, spiritual, and physical.

Emotional Needs: We have a deep need for friendship and love. The need is so great that even Jesus needed His close friends with Him when He was facing his deepest difficulty. Right before His arrest, He asked His disciples to stay and pray with Him for a while. Then He took three of His closest friends (Peter, and the two sons of Zebedee), a little further into the garden. I believe He desperately needed their friendship and love to give Him strength to face the horrors of what was coming next.

During the 3 years Jesus was ministering and teaching on Earth, He was clear about how He felt about friendships and true love. He commanded us to love one another. He demonstrated His love for you by laying down His life for your sins. He loves you so much He put it down in history that He considers you a friend!

"My command is this: Love each other as I have loved you."
John 15:12

"Greater love has no on than this: to lay down one's life for one's friends."
John 15:13

"You are my friends if you do what I command. I no longer call you servants, because a servant does not know his master's business. Instead, I have called you friends, for everything that I learned from my Father I have made known to you."
John 15:14

Just as Jesus needed earthly friends, you also need true friends. You also need the love of family...either blood family or loved ones you see as family. It is important to cultivate those relationships and make them as strong as you can. If you have already opened yourself up to them, these are the people who know you best. They know your likes, dislikes, talents, successes, mistakes, and generally what makes you tick.

Keep these people close. Never let a romantic relationship pull you away from your friends and family. When you start a relationship with someone, listen to the feedback of your trusted family and friends. They may see something in your relationship as a sign that this relationship is not healthy. If you've developed a good relationship with your family and friends, you should trust them if they have some concerns. Remember, they know you better than your boyfriend does. And, if your relationship fails for any reason, you should have your friends and family to run to for comfort and healing.

I've seen too many girls run headfirst into a relationship and leave faithful friends and family behind. I've seen them ignore warnings believing that they are right in "standing by their man." They do not feel that they have love and support from anyone, and they blame their families because of their disapproval of the relationship. But, when they first started dating, they should have leaned on the wisdom and advice from those who have "been there, done that." If they had, not only would they have avoided some bad relationships, but they would also have been fulfilled by the love from their family and friends. They wouldn't need to constantly look for fulfillment in the next relationship, as their lives would be complete without a man involved.

For a while, these girls felt justified by their actions and a sense of excitement and strength...until the relationship went south. Some of the girls who have gone through this cycle over and over no longer have the support of family or friends in any relationship. They're broken and needy. As soon as one relationship is over, they rush off to another one and the cycle begins all over again.

Take time to find your fulfillment in God. Let Him make you complete. Then He will bring along a man who is already complete to make your life gloriously full.

> *No matter how wonderful he is, no man is capable of "completing you" only God can do that.*

Spiritual Needs: A need for purpose and meaning is ingrained so deep in us that we spend our entire existence trying to discover what our purpose is on Earth and what the meaning of life is for us. Good news! You can stop wondering! I know the answer to both of those questions. We were created by a loving God to be His children. Our purpose was to love Him back and want a relationship with Him. The meaning of life is to reconnect with our Creator in our own unique way. Because of sin on Earth which separates humanity from their Creator, our other purpose is to do whatever we can with the talents, positions, and resources God has given us to bring this good news to everyone who will listen.

God created us to be perfect. We messed that up by sinning. After we messed up, He made a plan so that we can return to Him and allow Him to bring us back to a place of perfection because of His grace and mercy.

> *"For He chose us in Him before the creation of the world to be holy and blameless in His sight. In love He predestined us for adoption to be His children through Jesus Christ, in accordance with His pleasure and will."*
> *Ephesians 1:4-5*

The most important relationship we can ever have is our relationship with God. Did you know that He is jealous for you? He created you and He loves you! When the world pulls you away from Him, it breaks His heart. He wants the best for you, and He knows you're not going to find fulfillment in this world. Jesus came to catch our attention and let us know that God will do anything to win our hearts back from the pull of the world's distractions. When He returned to Heaven, he sent us the Holy Spirit to be our guide in day-to-day living.

If you cultivate your relationship with God and make it the most important relationship in your life, the Holy Spirit will be able to help you navigate all of your relationships. You'll know if your friendships and romantic relationships are healthy, need work, or simply need to be ended. The Holy Spirit will guide you to the right man and help you to build a relationship based on Godly principles, giving you the best foundation for a good marriage.

Physical Needs: Our bodies have a need to be provided for. We need air, food, water, sleep, and cleanliness. But, if we only got those things, we would not survive long. Did you know that without physical touch and comfort, it is possible to get sick and die? Friendships and love are vitally important for our physical health. Providing for our physical bodies is necessary for survival. It's also something that God promises to take care of as long as we keep our focus on Him.

"So do not worry, saying, "what shall we eat?" or "What shall we drink?" or "What shall we wear?" For the pagans run after all these things, and your Heavenly Father knows that you need them. But seek first His Kingdom and His righteousness, and all these things will be given to you as well.

Therefore, do not worry about tomorrow, for tomorrow will worry about itself. Each day has enough trouble of its own."
Matthew 6:31-34

So, where do our sexual "needs" fit in this equation? Well, that's an interesting question. The truth is that although we do need physical touch and affection to be healthy, sexual satisfaction is not actually necessary to physically live a healthy life. Many people have lived their entire lives without sexual satisfaction and have thrived.

Don't get me wrong, sex is an important part of a marriage relationship, and without sexual satisfaction in a marriage, the marriage could suffer. It is an incredibly important subject to cover because sex is the most passionate, most vulnerable, most intimate act a couple can perform. It produces life in a relationship, and very real physical life when a baby is conceived.

Believe it or not, sex takes up an incredibly small amount of married life. One study done by Newsweek suggests that a married couple might have sex 68 times a year on average. Since there are 365 days in a year, that's only 17% of an entire year of your life (give or take) depending on your life circumstances and your sexual drive as a couple. And it's even less than that, since each one of those days is 24 hours, and time spent actually having sex is typically less than a half an hour. That's 0.39% of an entire year.

So, what do married people do with the rest of the 99.61% of the year? Life. Pure and simple. Working jobs, building families, taking care of the home, the yard, the car, children, eating, sleeping, hopefully having vacation time together, watching TV, spending time together… Life. That is a big reason why saving sex for marriage is so important. You need to be so sure that you've found the right match for you that when life gets hard and sex happens less than 0.39% of the time, it won't hurt your marriage.

> *"Since sex actually takes up such a small percentage of our lives, why does society make it out to be the most important reason people get together?"*

Why has Hollywood glorified sexual drive and physical attraction as the most valuable part of a relationship? Why is it that as soon as a couple find out they are "meant for each other," they end up in bed? Because it's exciting for the big screen. Because writing every story around the ups and downs of life and relationships is boring. Because writing the script so that the couple has sex on their first date keeps the story moving when the producers have so little screen time to write the story. But most importantly, it's the enemy's plan to try to keep us distracted from truly connecting with people the way God planned it. His goal is always to derail God's will for our lives, and most of the time he does it in ways designed for us not to notice. He puts this big exciting romantic bait in front of our eyes and works to convince us that THIS is what we live for.

> *"Aren't I allowed to want things too?"*

YES! Let's talk about your wants. When you put your full trust in God and trust that He knows what you need better than you do, you will begin to discover the difference between what you really need, and what you simply want. When you identify those, you can start to see which wants are actually worth striving for.

If we didn't have things we want in life, we would never have any drive to work toward anything exciting. All of our attention would be focused on satisfying our immediate needs. When it comes to satisfaction, like I said before, it's ok to want things. We are designed to enjoy "things." So don't worry. I'm not saying you need to give up your cell phone, your makeup, or your favorite teddy bear which you will never part with but don't want anyone to know about. Go ahead and enjoy that occasional chocolate bar, Skittles, or cake. We are designed to satisfy our needs, and God also enjoys pleasure, so it's ok to satisfy some of our wants as well.

We just need to make sure that in satisfying those wants we are not hurting ourselves or others which would be stepping outside God's will for our lives. For instance, it's fine to want sweets, and even to indulge from time to time, but if you indulge too much, you will find yourself unhealthy, overweight, and possibly dealing with worse medical complications like diabetes or rotting teeth. Success is a good thing to want and strive for, but if you want success too much, you'll find yourself overworked, tired, and losing your most valuable relationships.

Life is about balance. If you keep your focus on God, He can help you sort out what's important and not important. He can help you prioritize your wants and needs in a healthy way. He can even help you to shift some of your desires to more healthy and successful options.

> *"Delight yourself in the Lord and He will give you the desires of your heart."*
> *Psalm 37:4*

No, this does not mean that if you go to church and sing and dance, He will give you that convertible you've had your eye on. It means that the more you focus on God, the more He can show you the better things in life. He can point you to things that really will satisfy you, and then give you the strength and plan to go after and actually obtain those things.

***"Since we need love, isn't it ok to want to find
a boyfriend to fill that need?"***

Sure, it's ok to do that. But the love that you're looking for is not going to be found in a boyfriend. Only God can love you in the deep way that you're looking for. Allow God to fill that emptiness in your heart, and He will also help you to mature to the point that you don't need a boyfriend to make you feel complete. God's desire is for you to realize that you do not need a man to make you feel loved, accepted, and beautiful. When you finally reach that place, you'll realize that a man does not complete you ... God does.

Then, when God does bring along Prince Charming, your relationship will be built on a strong foundation. You will not need each other to make your lives complete. Instead, your lives will be more full because you have each other. Who wants to settle for just what you need when you can have so much more?

Imagine you and your future husband each build half a house. Put it together, and you have a complete house, right? But when you put the two halves together, you may realize that not all the walls line up. You may end up with half your bedroom connected to the kitchen! Great for a midnight snack, but not so great for privacy. You'll end up needing to knock some walls down and build some others up to make your two half houses fit together. Also, until you meet, you both must live in just half a house. How are you going to survive with missing walls ... maybe a missing bathroom? ... Who has the kitchen until your houses are connected? ... Maybe not the most well thought out plan.

I'm not saying that two half-built people can't build a home together. But maybe God has a better plan in mind so that you don't have to spend the first few years of your marriage remodeling.

Imagine you and God build a complete house, and your future husband does the same. When you each build your house with God, He has the plans for both houses and knows how they will fit together once you two meet. In the meantime, you have a full house to live in. Safe, secure, and it has everything you need. And the best part is, when you do put your houses together, and knock down those temporary walls which were built to protect you for your future spouse, you'll end up with a mansion!

So, instead of being envious of someone else's relationship, take the time to build your house using God's plans. When you do, you will build something so beautiful others will look at your life and say, "I want something like that!" Then you can share with them how you and God built your life and how they can do it too.

Love Does Not Boast/ is not Proud

Chapter 7

Boast - Verb: 'talk with excessive pride and self-satisfaction about one's achievements, possessions, or abilities'

Pride - Noun: 'the quality of having an excessively high opinion of oneself or one's importance.'

My Story

I made some very dear friends and after college I got a job at a private Christian school, but after a couple of years God told me to "Go back home." Home? Go home to my tiny little town where there are few good men and even fewer opportunities? I loved my family and dearly missed my friends, but I was making a life for myself out there! I was supposed to meet my future husband out here and get married! Going home felt like a step backward in life.

He kept urging me, "Go home."

I fought with Him for two weeks (I don't recommend doing that). I finally made plans and moved home. It was a very humbling experience. I went from being on my own with my own apartment and a good job at a church/school to living back at home with my mom. Honestly, it was embarrassing, and I had no idea what God was thinking. Little did I know that the next few years would be so precious for me! God knew exactly what He was doing.

I had the privilege of watching as my mom and dad re-built a broken relationship and then re-marry after 13 years apart. I watched them learn how to respect each other, set boundaries, and make it to their second wedding day without even kissing! Apparently, this goal was inspired by me and my determination for my first kiss to be on my wedding day.

I started my own sewing and alterations business out of my brother's thrift store. I worked there for a while, but never really made enough to make ends meet, so I got a job at a local grocery store to save money and buy a car because my old car had broken down on my move back home.

So, I was in my early 20s, living at home with my parents, and didn't have a car. I really felt that I had taken a huge step back in my adulthood. It was a humbling experience, but I was still glad that my parents were there for me and didn't mind supporting me until I figured out what God wanted me to do next.

God's View on Pride

"God opposes the proud but gives grace to the humble."
Proverbs 3:34

We're not talking about being proud of ourselves or our accomplishments. Being proud of ourselves and each other is important for our mental and physical health. Those are good things! God is proud of us when we listen to the Holy Spirit's lead and when we make good decisions for our lives. He's proud of us when we share His love with others, when we forgive those who have done wrong against us, and when we pursue the good things He has laid out for us to do. He is proud to be our Father when we humble ourselves and give up our pride to be His children.

When it says that God opposes the proud, it's talking about prideful hearts. It was pride that caused Satan to believe that he could elevate himself to be greater than God. It was pride that deceived Eve into taking the fruit in the Garden because she thought it would make her "like God." Story, after story, after story throughout the Bible tells of people who allowed pride to get in the way of relationships, put lives in danger, killed people, and effected entire civilizations.

God opposes the proud because it hurts His people.

Pride in Friendships

Take a minute to be really honest with yourself. Do you find yourself dominating most conversations because there is so much you know about the topic that you can't help but share? Do you tend to feel that you have more to offer a relationship, friendship, or subject than others do? Perhaps you are prideful. Are you the kind of person who brags about yourself or your accomplishments? Do you feel that you need to make yourself look good to others because you don't feel very good about yourself? When you see other people succeed, do you find yourself trying to find flaws in them or downplaying their accomplishments because you can't see yourself ever reaching the goals they have reached? Do you feel that you will never be as smart as they are? Do you feel you will never have the "perfect" family or relationship that they have?

If so, there is something wrong with your perspective. You are trying to compare two totally different people and completely different lives. It's like trying to compare a carrot to a banana. Is a carrot better than a banana because it's higher in vitamin E? Is a banana better than a carrot because it has a lot of potassium? Absolutely not! Each food is valuable all by itself. Each food has a lot to add to someone's health. A banana might be sweeter than a carrot, but a banana would taste awful if dipped in ranch dressing.

Having good self-esteem doesn't mean you are naturally prideful. And, it is possible to have low self-esteem and be prideful. Pride is a matter of the heart. It's a sense that you are in some ways better than someone else. You may not like the way you look, but at least you don't dress like 'that girl.' You may not be the smartest person in the world, but at least you don't goof off in class like 'that guy.'

The Bible gives this example about pride in the parable of the pharisee and the tax collector:

> "To some who were confident of their own righteousness and looked down on everyone else, Jesus told this parable: "Two men went up to the temple to pray, one a Pharisee and the other a tax collector. The Pharisee stood by himself and prayed: 'God, I thank you that I am not like other people – robbers, evildoers, adulterers – or even like this tax collector. I fast twice a week and give a tenth of all I get.'
>
> But the tax collector stood at a distance. He would not even look up to heaven, but beat his chest and said, "God, have mercy on

me, a sinner.' " "I tell you that this man, rather than the other, went home justified before God. For all those who exalt themselves will be humbled, and those who humble themselves will be exalted."

Luke 18:9-14

Pride is a very dangerous trait that gets us into a lot of trouble. When we're prideful, God says that He will not justify us (forgive our sins). But don't worry, you're not alone. Everyone deals with pride. It's a constant struggle to overcome the feeling that we are better than others because of how we look, live, dress, act, speak… you name it. We naturally judge people based on our first impression of them. Then we size them up to see if they are better or worse than ourselves. It might be due to the way they dress, where they live, what look they have on their face, what grades they get, how they style their hair, how old they are…

Pre-judging is our natural way to assess the world around us and can be very helpful in keeping us safe in certain situations. It is very important to be cautious when you sense something "off" about someone. But, we tend to let those pre-judgments determine where people stand in society, allowing us the opportunity to put ourselves and others into rankings and positions. That's when it turns into prejudice or racism.

Prejudice and racism are both born out of pride. Millions of people have been enslaved, tortured, assaulted, and killed because of pride. Because someone thought they and their "kind" were better than someone else and their "kind." This is a dangerous view to have on God's creation, because these people will answer to the Creator Himself on how they've treated His creation.

God calls us to something greater than that. He did not create any person to be more important than anyone else. He did not make any one person more valuable than anyone else, and it is time we start to see that. It's time to get over ourselves.

"So, how do I overcome pride?"

"Do nothing out of selfish ambition or vain conceit. Rather, in humility value others above yourselves, not looking to your own interests but each of you to the interests of others."
Philippians 2:3-4

It's exhausting to try to keep up with everyone. You can't please everyone, and no matter how hard you try you will never reach anyone's standards of perfection. All you will do is wear yourself out. You were never meant to be just like everyone else. They weren't either! Each person was specifically designed by God to be unique and to offer the world something different. You have so much to offer just by being you. And what you have to offer is not more or less valuable than what someone else has to offer… It's just different.

So, start by asking God to show you what you look like through His eyes. Build up your self-esteem so that when others compliment you, it feels good to know that other see in you the qualities the God has given you.

God is the only one who can help you see your self-worth. God is the only one who knows all of those wonderful qualities He has put in you and how you can use each one to make the world a better place. When you learn to see life from God's perspective, you won't need to try to see flaws in others in order to make yourself look good and feel better about yourself. You'll feel good about yourself because you will actually see value in yourself.

Look outside yourself. Look at the world around you. Try to see others the way God does. Try to put yourself in their shoes. See what they see. Even if you don't agree with someone's point of view, you might be able to at least understand how they got to their conclusions. Even if you don't agree with the choices they've made, maybe you can at least see why they made them.

There's a saying, "People don't care how much you know until they know how much you care." I believe Jesus lived this way. He cared for people by helping them, healing them, making them feel special and important. When it came time for him to talk, they listened! We should be like this. When we believe in God, and have decided to follow Jesus' teaching, our world no longer revolves around ourselves. We need to look beyond ourselves and see how we can impact those around us. We can make this world a better place by putting our pride down and caring for others the way we want to be cared for.

Pride Destroys Relationships

Have you ever heard someone talk about how good they've got it? Maybe someone talks all the time about how their parents give them everything they want. Someone else is doing well in school and is rubbing it in how their grades are better than anyone else in their class. Maybe a girl is bragging about how her boyfriend keeps giving her gifts. Maybe a guy is telling everyone how his girl will have sex with him. (Yes, girls, they do that... even when it's not true)

People like this leave the impression that they are full of themselves, selfish, inconsiderate, never think of other's feelings, or think that they are better than anyone else.

If someone is boastful, their focus is on themselves and making themselves look good or feel more important. A self-focused person is not the kind of person you want to get into a relationship with…especially romantically. These people don't have time to care about others properly because their attention is always on themselves and what makes them happy. This means that they won't care about you or making you happy but will expect you to care about them and keeping them happy.

Boastful people have a hard time loving others because they don't love themselves or are so full of themselves that they don't have time to love anyone else.

When someone is self-focused, it doesn't always mean that they think highly of themselves. In fact, it usually means that they are broken, hurt, scared, or depressed. A person like this cannot see beauty or worth in themselves. They overcompensate for their lack of self-esteem by looking to others to make them feel better about themselves or their lives. They brag about themselves in order to get that desired attention and ego boost.

Let's look at some possible reasons that someone is boastful.

- The person who truly thinks that he is better than anyone else. This person simply doesn't care about others and is incapable of real love.
- The person whose parents give her everything she wants. Maybe her parents aren't around much or are going through a divorce. Maybe they're trying to make her feel better about her home situation by buying her more stuff. – News Flash: It doesn't work. She will brag about her possessions because she is trying to overcompensate for how lonely she is and how much pain she is in. This person needs to find forgiveness for her parents before she will be able to learn

how to love properly.
- The person bragging about good grades may be flat-out lying in order to hide the fact that he's struggling in school. Maybe he is getting good grades but only because of the immense pressure he is under. He feels that if he doesn't get good grades, he'll never measure up to his parent's standards, or his own. Maybe he finds his identity in his grades because he doesn't find it anywhere else. Maybe he's cheating because he really doesn't get it and is ashamed to ask for help. A person like this will need to focus on maturing and handling life before he can learn how to properly cultivate a relationship.
- The girl bragging about all the gifts her boyfriend gets her could actually be a victim of abuse by her boyfriend who gives her the gifts to keep her quiet. Perhaps she's too scared to come forward. Maybe she's bragging about him to hide what's going on and keep him happy in an effort to keep his abuse at bay. A person like this will need to learn that no form of abuse is an acceptable form of love. She will need to learn how to become independent of all relationships and learn how to truly love herself before she will be capable of truly loving someone else.
- The guy who talks about having sex with his girlfriend might be lying about it. Maybe he isn't really having sex with her, but his friends have made him feel that if he's not having sex, he's not a real man. And if he is having sex with her, he's bragging about it because it makes him feel cool in front of his friends. Real love would not be bragging about such a personal aspect of life in order to make himself more acceptable to his friends. Notice, the focus is on him and what he got out of the relationship. This guy needs to learn how to respect women as people and not pieces of property, or a piece of flesh to be used for his own personal gain. Until he does this, he is not capable of real love.

All of the above examples show people who have little self-esteem. These people will suck the life and energy out of you in an attempt to fill the need to feel good about themselves. If you decide to have a long relationship or close friendship with someone like this, you will find yourself putting more into the relationship than you get out of it. Eventually, you may wish you were more careful when you started hanging out with this person.

And please don't think that you can love the person long enough or hard enough to change this about them. You can't give someone self-esteem if they refuse to see value in themselves. This kind of person will only be able to see their own worth when they choose to see themselves through God's eyes. Until then, no number of compliments or encouragement will be enough. This kind of person will always need more and won't be satisfied.

I'm not saying don't be friends with people who have low self-esteem. If that were the case, most of you would have to stop being friends with yourself! What I am saying is choose your friends carefully and help them when you can but be careful that they don't drain all of your energy. Protect yourself, your heart, and your life. Offer them friendship, be there for them, and be a true and faithful friend, but set boundaries for yourself so that you don't burn out or find yourself stuck in situations where you are putting more into the relationship than you are getting out of it. You're not married to this person, you are not their parent, and they are not your responsibility. You cannot save them, only God can do that.

What I am saying is please don't get into a romantic relationship with someone who still has so much work to do on himself. A relationship is different than a friendship. In a relationship, you will be more easily hurt by a person whose focus is only on himself. In a friendship, if you need to walk away for a time, you can. It's a lot harder to do this in a relationship, especially if you become sexually active.

Boys are attracted to anything that makes them feel good and fulfills their needs. A real man will be attracted to your self-confidence and will appreciate the strong, valuable, talented woman you are becoming. Boys will ask, manipulate, and push you to get physical. A real man will respect you so much that he will not ask you to do anything that will damage your self-esteem, your reputation, or get you off track from doing what is best for your life.

When looking for good traits in a future husband, a healthy amount of self-confidence is a good thing to watch for. But when self-confidence turns into conceit or pride, watch out! When it comes to feelings, he may shove them deep down because he doesn't want to be considered weak. But, over time, feelings that are not dealt with will pressurize. If he doesn't have a healthy outlet, those feelings will eventually explode…probably all over you.

A prideful man will have difficulty admitting fault in many situations. During arguments, he tends to push his point way beyond what is reasonable only because he doesn't want to be proven wrong. His need to be right will begin to overtake his desire to care about your opinions and feelings. His world will probably revolve around himself, and he will likely expect that your world should revolve around him as well. He might begin to demand things of you. If so, your relationship will start to resemble a dictatorship rather than a partnership. This toxicity will work its way into your own spirit and destroy you, if you let it.

"Pride goes before destruction and a haughty spirit before a fall."
Proverbs 16:18

Look for a man of humility to spend the rest of your life with. A man who understands that he is nothing without God will always understand that your relationship is more important than his ego. He will know that it's ok to be wrong sometimes, and that other people's opinions and feelings have value.

> "Therefore, as God's chosen people Holy and dearly loved, clothe yourselves with compassion, kindness, humility, gentleness, and patience."
> Colossians 3:12

Love is Not Rude

Chapter 8

Noun: 'offensively impolite or ill mannered.'

My Story

Here, I must go back a few months to my brother's wedding. Apparently, his bride had a friend who had recently become a Christian and was looking for a godly woman to marry. My future sister-in-law had told him about me, and he wanted to meet me. So, at their wedding he asked me to dance. We talked a little, but I wasn't finding myself completely smitten. He was nice, and good looking, but I just wasn't sure. There were a few small things about his personality that I just didn't connect with.

He was a touch overwhelming for me. He had a very outgoing personality and exuded confidence, but I think that's what kind of turned me off. It was almost as if he expected me to like him as much as he liked me. My brother had given him my phone number, and he started texting me. At that time in history, texts were not free, and I had a limited number of texts I could send and receive. I had to tell him as much and ask him to stop texting before I went over and was charged for the texts. Plus, I didn't exactly like that he had my phone number without asking me himself if it would be ok to call. So, he stopped calling and texting for the time being. But he didn't give up easily.

After I moved back home, my brother encouraged him to get involved in a discipleship program a few hours away from my home. This would help him grow in God and give us an opportunity to get to know each other better. He would not be allowed to date during his internship, but I could still go down and get involved in an outreach here and there and he would come up to my town to visit from time to time.

At the time, I was working at the grocery store saving money to buy my car. One evening I was working the check stand, and a couple of young men came through my line to buy milk and donuts. What stood out to me was that one of these young men was wearing a "goofy grin" and carrying a small Bible nuzzled in the crook of his arm. ... more on that later.

Near the end of his year internship, I had thought that I was in love with the man from Florida and was ready to take the next step of becoming boyfriend/girlfriend after he graduated. I had even decided to go ahead and get my drawing of my wedding dress made into real gown by a local seamstress that my mom had discovered.

About a week before graduation, I got a call from this man informing me that God had told him not to date for a while longer. The conversation was ambiguous enough that I really wasn't sure what that meant. I retreated to my "spot" in the hills and had a conversation with God about it. "Am I supposed to wait for him?" "Is this you saying I need to move on?" "How am I supposed to handle this?" God wasn't clear with me, but I later discovered that He was protecting me, my heart, and my desire to not date until I found the man I was going to marry.

What God Says About Rudeness

The Bible is full of scriptures that talk about God's desire for how we treat one another. From honoring parents to treating others as better than ourselves and loving our enemies. It's clear that God wants us to have good and solid relationships. You may have heard of the Golden Rule. "Do to others as you would have them do to you." This is from Scripture!

> *"So whatever you wish that others would do to you, do also to them, for this is the Law and the Prophets."*
> *Matthew 7:12*

If you wouldn't want someone to be rude to you, don't be rude to others. If you would rather someone understand where you're coming from in any given situation, you need to be understanding of where other people are coming from too... Even if you don't necessarily agree with them or what they did.

God calls us to do better... to be better. He commands us to pray for our enemies and those who wrong us. When we show kindness instead of rudeness, we are showing that we are willing to "be the bigger person."

> *"A soft answer turns away wrath, but a harsh word stirs up anger."*
> *Proverbs 15:1*

God is kind, loving, and gracious with us. We need to be no less to everyone around us.

"People are rude to me all the time! How do I handle it?"

You know the obviously rude ones. They are the bullies. They talk down about someone else's appearance, intelligence, or even their hobbies or likes. They are not hard to find. They're everywhere. If you have siblings, you probably experience rudeness on a daily basis. Even you have probably been rude from time to time.

Being rude seems so harmless when you're the one doing it. You know that you didn't really mean what you said, but your emotions got the better of you. What they said or did just set you off. You just couldn't help yourself...Right? Well, that's not what it looks like from the other person's point of view. What if you were in that person's position? Would you forgive the other person as easily as you do yourself? Would you justify their rudeness the way you do yours? Probably not.

> *"If you don't have anything nice to say, don't say anything at all."*
> *"Treat others like you want to be treated."*

Notice the saying is not, "Treat others like they treat you." When someone is mean or rude to you, it doesn't justify you being mean or rude back. It doesn't matter if someone is rude to you, God still calls you to be kind back. This doesn't mean "don't stand up for yourself," or "let people walk all over you." It simply means, don't stoop to their level. Be the better person. Walk away if you need to. If you stoop to their level, you're just becoming like them.

> *"Don't answer the foolish arguments of fools, or you will become as foolish as they are."*
> *Proverbs 26:4*

Take a minute to think about this...What is your normal response when someone calls you stupid? Normally it falls somewhere along the lines of, "I'm not stupid, You're stupid." Or, if you're anything like I was, you start to cry. How does that work out for you? Does it stop the bullying? Usually, it makes it worse, because the other person has gained power. They started it...they have confidence...and they got to you.

What if, instead, you turned it into a joke and agreed with them?

Them: "You're stupid!"
You: "Yeah, I can be pretty dumb sometimes!"
Them: A little stunned, "Yea, … you are."
You: With a smile, "you're pretty smart for noticing." You've just turned it back around on them by appealing to their vanity.
Them: "…"

What can they say? Thank you? You have just taken back all the power without playing their game or being rude. At this point, you hold all the cards and have taken the wind out of their sails. You are free to befriend them, change the subject, or walk away. The game is yours now.

For the math minded people, it is simple math.
Start with 0. Subtract 1 (their negative comment). React by subtracting 1 again (your negative response). You end up with negative 2 (an all-negative situation).

Now start with 0. Subtract 1 (their negative comment). React by adding 1 (your positive reaction). You end up back at 0. You've neutralized the negative situation. If they keep subtracting, you keep adding and bringing it back to 0. If you get a chance to 1 up the positive, you'll end up with a positive situation! It's so much easier to produce positive things to say than negative. All you have to do is start complimenting them. Their hair, their shoes, their nicely manicured nails, a talent you know they have… The possibilities are endless.

When you learn to grasp how much incredible power this method has, you will not only be able to stand up for yourself, but you will also have tough enough skin to stand up for someone else.

Being rude doesn't have to be a default reaction. Being kind should be our default. Not because it is weakness, but because kindness holds so much more power than rudeness. When used properly, love is infinitely more powerful than hate.

For the record, I'm only speaking to vocal bullying here. Physical violence should be handled much differently. We will discuss that more later.

Rudeness Has No Place in Relationships

I think we can all agree that being rude is not a quality we want in ourselves, our friends, or our romantic relationships, but how do we make sure that the guy we like is a respectful guy? For starters, determine not to get into a relationship with someone you don't really know well. "He likes me" or "he's cute" does not mean he's good enough for you. "He's always nice to me" does not mean that he is always respectful to everyone. Of course he's nice to you! He's pursuing you for a romantic relationship. Being rude would be a bad idea if you're wanting to get on a girl's good side.

How does he talk about his friends? Is he respectful to them, or are they always talking down to each other? Even in joking, talking negatively about someone is rude. When done in excess, it is a huge warning sign. How does he talk about teachers? Does he make fun of them? Does he talk negatively about their intelligence, how they dress, what car they drive? Red flags, girls. Even not talking about someone at all is better than talking rudely. How about his parents or his siblings? Does he talk about them like he likes them?

When someone around him is rude, how does he react? Does he join in the rudeness? Does he laugh because he wants to fit in, or does he do something to neutralize the negative remark? Even allowing rudeness to go on around you is rude even if you're not actively joining in. Think about it. If someone said something rude about you, what would your best friend do? You'd better believe she'd stand up for you! You should expect nothing less from a romantic relationship. He should be able to stand up for himself, you, and others if someone is being rude.

If the guy you're considering dating is not respectful of others, he will not respect you. Even if he's nice and respectful at first, he won't be able to hold that disguise for very long. As soon as your relationship comes to the point that you start arguing about things, he will begin to disrespect you.

Name calling frequently comes up in arguments when a rude person is involved. Name calling has no place in a healthy relationship. When arguments arise, it's natural for us to be angry and want to lash back at our opponent. But name calling is counterproductive and won't solve the argument. It will only serve to make matters worse. There's a real issue that needs to be dealt with, but instead, you're attacking each other personally. This never ends well.

Instead, bite your tongue. Stay on topic. Deal with the actual issue and do not disrespect each other. Many times, you'll find that the issue was more of a misunderstanding. If you have any chance of resolving the misunderstanding, DO NOT let name calling become part of the discussion. Remember, your opponent is not actually the other person. It's the issue that needs to be resolved. If you can keep your focus on the issue, you can save each other a lot of pain and frustration.

When it comes to physical boundaries, a rude person will only be able to hold off for a little while. Eventually, his physical desire will become stronger than any agreement you have made. He will begin to push those boundaries. He might start making fun of how "uptight" you are. He may jokingly call you a "prude."

He may start making comments about your body which make you uncomfortable. He may start touching you in inappropriate places and then say, "I was only joking. Relax."

Don't relax. Don't take the rudeness for even one minute. Stand up for yourself and get out of the situation. This is not the type of guy you want to have in your life. He does not respect you, he won't respect your friends or family, and he won't respect your relationship or the boundaries you have set.

Respect is the key word here. Look for a man who is respectful to everyone around him. A guy who opens doors for you is good, but a guy who opens doors for others is better. A guy who respects your parents is good, but a guy who respects his own parents just as much is better. A guy who is friendly to your friends is good, but a guy who is friendly to strangers is better. A guy who stands up for his friends is good, but a guy who will stand up for anyone is better.

Look for someone who is generous, respectful, and helpful. That is the kind of guy whose world does not revolve around himself. He thinks about others first. He will put your needs above his own. And, if you're putting his needs above your own as well, you will find yourself in a balanced relationship.

Love is Not Self Seeking

Chapter 9

Adjective: 'having concern for one's own welfare and interests before those of others.'

My Story

The evening after the conversation with the man I was so sure God had for me, I went to our church's young adult meeting. I was still distraught and didn't talk to too many people, including the "new guy," who turned out to be the guy with the goofy grin from the grocery store, although I did not realize it at the time.

Fast-forward 3 months. My parents had remarried and were preparing to move from the house I grew up in to "The Ranch." This was a house my dad bought way up in the mountains. My brother had invited the "new guy" over for lunch after church one Sunday. He hadn't been to church since the Young Adult meeting, and my brother wanted to be welcoming. When my mom discovered that he lived in the same mountain community we were moving to, she hired him on the spot to help us move and help with some work on the garage up there. He readily agreed. She was always looking to hire young people who were looking for side work and needed a leg up.

Over the next few months, I got to know this guy. His name was Frankie. He was funny, sweet, loved God, and was passionate about the truth of the Bible. We began to become good friends. We started having long conversations about life and God, and genuinely enjoyed spending time together as friends.

I was still waiting for God to give me clear direction about the guy from Florida I had been getting to know over the past year and had come to realize that I was not actually "in love" with him. I was in love with the "idea" of him. My mom thought it was a cute idea and my sister-in-law was the one who was trying to set us up. The power of suggestion is a powerful thing. I thought that since they approved, and that he was the first man who had shown genuine interest in me, maybe he was "the one." So, I fooled myself into thinking I was falling in love with him, but always had this feeling at the back of my heart that I was settling.

Just a month or two after he had told me that God didn't want him to date for a while, I realized I wasn't that interested in him. I just needed God to give me closure. Finally, I received a call from him. He explained to me that he had found someone else. I was so relieved! I had the closure I needed to put that whole situation behind me. He pursued me and I selfishly took the bait because it felt good to be wanted and pursued.

Maybe he lost interest because I was putting him off until the end of his internship, or maybe he just built a friendship with his other girl and realized he was falling for her instead of me. Maybe he decided to tell me that God wanted him to not date for a while because he was embarrassed to tell me that he had found someone else or because he didn't want to hurt my feelings and wanted to let me down easy. I may never know. But it doesn't really matter. While I had gotten emotionally invested in this guy, I had never made a close connection with him, so when I finally got that closure, it was easy to let it go.

God and Selfishness

If you have not caught the concept earlier in this book, catch it now: GOD is the ONLY one who can fulfill those needs and desires you have inside you. I know you may not believe it. Most people don't. But I promise it's true. If my husband were to die, I would be devastated and I would miss him terribly, but I would continue to live on. My life wouldn't suddenly end because his did. GOD is my reason for living. HE fulfills every need and desire I have. I am HIS daughter first and a wife to my husband second. When you understand your place in the Kingdom of God, you will find that your need for a man to fill your desires will fade.

Dear daughter of the King,
Don't think that your man is your only reason for living.
That's not his purpose. And it's not yours.
You each have a very significant and separate
role to play in this world.
Find your purpose.
Let your future husband find his purpose.
Then, when God brings you together, your purpose will
Be made that much more adventurous.

Real love is a two-way street. Real love thinks about what is best for the other person.

"Do not be concerned about your own interests, but also be concerned about the interests of others."
Philippians 2:4

When you understand that sex is God's beautiful gift designed for marriage, and that having sex before marriage robs you and your partner of the true beauty of that gift, you won't want to take that gift away from your partner. Temporary pleasure isn't worth losing the beauty of pure love.

Selfishness is a Relationship Killer

If we are being honest, selfishness is the reason most people look for someone to have a relationship with. We are lonely. We are afraid of being alone. We want someone to love us and tell us we are beautiful. We want someone to think we are worth fighting for. We do not want to be the only one without someone. We want a distraction from our problems. Well, guess what? Most guys are looking for someone for the same reasons (and a few more). They are not actually looking for YOU. You are both looking for someone to fulfill a need or desire you have inside of you, but if you're being honest with yourselves, the "who" does not really matter as much as it should.

I hope you can see that putting the interests of your future husband, children, and even yourself before your immediate desire for affection and acceptance really does serve you better overall. Putting others first puts you in a great position for a happy and fulfilling life, marriage, and family.

Now, we're going to get real about a touchy subject - pornography. You may or may not have seen something pornographic by this point in your life, but there is a good chance that you will at some point. I want to expose pornography for what it really is so that you are fully aware of the dangers of pornography for everyone involved.

The average age a person is exposed to pornography is widely documented at 11 years old. But there are also children being exposed at 9 years old and even younger. Can you imagine your kid sister or kid brother watching porn? What would you do if you saw this happening? I sincerely hope you would put a stop to it.

Pornography is one of the most self-seeking things a person can get themselves involved in. It is very addictive, and way too many teens have gotten caught up in the addiction. They watch it when their brains are still developing, and chemical reactions occur in the brain which then re-wires the brain so that it demands more. Just as any addiction, the addict will become less and less satisfied with smaller amounts or "milder" porn and begin to seek more exciting things to satisfy the need for a "fix." They typically become increasingly dissatisfied with what they are getting. After a while, their attention starts to turn toward the "real deal." They will begin to expect pornographic acts from their relationship. If they are not satisfied that their girlfriend/boyfriend is doing a good enough job, they may become more demanding or violent. If they aren't in a romantic relationship, they may begin to look for ways to take advantage of someone else. If a person like this does not get help, when they get older, they may get involved in the pornography and/or sex trafficking industries.

There are other side effects of porn addiction. Someone who is addicted to porn may have poor concentration because their mind is so consumed with sex and porn. They may have low motivation for doing things like doing well in school or sports. The addiction keeps calling them, so they become less interested in doing things normal people their age enjoy. Depression can come on for many reasons, but addiction to pornography can also be a factor. Someone who is deeply addicted can end up with social anxiety. Their view of sex is not the only thing effected. Their view of the world around them, and other people can become distorted, so being around groups of people make them very nervous. Because of the high demand for porn stars to be perfect, negative self-perception is a huge side effect. Guys can also get erectile dysfunction from porn addiction. Their bodies become accustomed to a certain type of "satisfaction," which means that other forms of "satisfaction" will not satisfy anymore.

Pre-teens and teens who have watched porn are more likely

to have a distorted view of what sex is supposed to be about. Which is unfortunate, especially since that is one of the main reasons a teen will watch porn to begin with. Most people will start watching porn because they are curious, and because it's exciting to try something you aren't supposed to be doing. When they watch porn, boys tend to think that this is what sex should be like, and girls think that this is what is expected of them. But pornography is NOT an adequate example of how sex is performed. It is acted and exaggerated, and the point is to make people interested and curious…as well as addicted. The more they can keep people interested, the more people will buy.

There have been reports from those who have been in the porn industry describing their job as "awkward, uncomfortable," and downright "painful." The women are more likely to be put in uncomfortable positions than the men. This doesn't sound like such a great job, does it?

Even those who do it as a legitimate job are in danger. They have to be tested for STDs every single month, and if they do have an STD, they're out of work until it's cleared up. And think about it…If they get an STD during that month, they can pass it to others before they're tested again. Some of the STDs can be cured with time or medication. Others will stay with them for the rest of their lives. Still others can cost them their lives.

There are other dangers as well. There are certain sexual acts that are performed for pornography that are downright dangerous to the body. There can be tearing and bleeding, and even if those don't happen, there is a lot of pain involved with these kinds of acts. In addition, some sexual acts that don't necessarily spread STDs can still spread bacteria's, viruses, and infections that can be life threatening.

Fact: Most sexual predators start out dabbling in pornography

The pornography industry is filled with men (yes, men), women, and children who are coerced or forced into it. Sure, there are some who have chosen to work in the porn industry as an actual job, but they are not safe from the dangers of it either. The fact is that pornography is an industry that brings in billions of dollars per year and feeds human trafficking and sex slavery. Slaves who are forced to perform sex acts against their will to fill the pockets of their slaveowners. And we're not talking about a few people here and there. We're talking about millions of people who have been forced into sexual exploitation. Almost all of them are female and a frightening number of them are children under the age of 16. Many of them were runaways who were coerced into the trade by people they trusted to give them help.

Does this make you want to cry...or be sick to your stomach? The pornography industry is full of victims of sex trafficking. In addition, pornography is shown to victims of sex trafficking as training videos so that the victim will learn how to perform those acts with "clients." Human trafficking and pornography feed off each other.

I think it's safe to say that sex trafficking for pornography is directly connected to the fact that there aren't enough "porn stars" who will willingly put themselves through this kind of torture. The market for pornography is too great for porn directors and producers to keep up with the demand.

How do we fix this? First and foremost, stay away from pornography. Raise awareness. If we can expose pornography for what it is, and get more people to stay away from pornography, the demand will begin to decline. The less people buy, the less demand there will be. The less demand, the less need there will be for actors. The less need for actors, the less human trafficking will occur. Can we eradicate sex trafficking and/or pornography? Probably not. But, if one less person is pulled into the industry because more awareness was raised, don't you think it's worth trying?

Now that you understand the porn industry a little better, I hope you can see how dangerous it is. I hope that you will stay away from it yourself. And I hope that you will not tolerate pornography in your relationships.

But, how do you know if your boyfriend is watching porn? He may have trouble concentrating on good conversations with you. It's very likely that he will frequently crack sexual jokes and/or sexual movements. He may be more touchy with you than you are comfortable with. He will "undress you" with his eyes. These are good signs that his mind is consumed with sex and sexual acts, and it will come out in one way or another. Depression and low body image are also things to watch out for.

If your boyfriend consistently tries to push your boundaries or has a few "ideas" he would like you to try, it is a good bet he's been watching porn. He got those ideas from somewhere.

On the other hand, some people that are addicted to pornography are less and less interested in being intimate with their significant other. If his "needs" are being satisfied with pornography, he may start being less affectionate with you and seem more "distracted." But, the sexual jokes and inappropriate behavior will probably continue.

Being less affectionate may sound good, if you are trying to maintain your own purity. But remember this…if he's doing porn, his mind is not pure. If he's becoming more distant from you because he's being satisfied with his own addiction, he will never be able to be intimate with you properly. If he's adding to the porn industry, he's adding to the problem. He will be objectifying women and will not understand what a healthy relationship looks like.

Get away from a guy like this. Do not stay in a relationship with a porn addict. Don't stay in a relationship with anyone who feels that pornography "isn't that bad." Get out as quickly as you can. Tell him to get help for himself, then get as far away from him as you can.

Love is Not Easily Angered

Chapter 10

Verb: 'To be filled with annoyance, displeasure, or hostility.'

"But you, Lord, are a compassionate and gracious God, slow to anger, abounding in love and faithfulness."
Psalm 86:15

My Story

Frankie was going to college, and I started helping him with one of his art classes. I was a little more creative than him in the art department, and this was a required class. The night I received the call from the "Florida guy," I picked Frankie up to go to my house so we could work on some of those projects together. I told him about the phone call and how relieved I was (So was he, but I didn't know it at the time). I began to settle into a good friendship with Frankie, but I did not allow my heart to go any further than that for a few more months.

One evening, Frankie and I were at his parent's house working on a mosaic for his art class. I caught myself starting to flirt with him a little. Flirt? Me? The last poor attempt I had made at flirting was at my crush in high school, and that didn't go anywhere. I had built high protective walls around my heart, and they were starting to come down as I was connecting with my friend. Was I actually developing feelings for him? Was it actually ok?

I started talking to God about it. God wasn't saying no. The more time we spent getting to know each other, the more connected I felt with him. One night, Frankie had finished doing some work on "The Ranch," and my dad paid him and gave him some extra money for the two of us to go out and get dinner. Frankie took me to a nice little restaurant upriver. Since he did not officially ask me out, I did not consider that our first date, but after that, we did begin discussing our relationship. We discussed our relationship with my parents, and Frankie asked for my dad's blessing to begin to court his daughter. My dad declared that we were adults and could do what we wanted, but I know he was honored anyway.

It was almost immediately that our relationship was tested. Frankie had a past, and it wasn't pretty. I had known there were some lingering effects from his past, but I did not really understand the entirety of what I was getting into. He had told me part of the story, but not all of it. The elders in my church were also close family friends. They discussed his past with him and helped him to understand that he really needed to be open about his past and trust that God's people understood forgiveness and God's changing grace.

Frankie realized that if he was going to pursue a relationship with me, and possibly marry me, he would need to be completely open and honest with me about his past. He invited me out to dinner and told me he wanted to talk about something. Because I had such a close church family, I knew what he wanted to talk with me about. My mom had discussed it with me ahead of time and helped me to be prepared. She asked me what I would say to him. I told her that I would pray about it and decide what to say after we had our talk. I knew that God would speak to me and tell me if I should move forward with this relationship or back off.

Frankie took me out to dinner and told me his whole story. He was completely honest and vulnerable in sharing hard truths about who he was before Christ changed his life. I listened carefully and prayerfully. I asked questions and searched my spirit for confirmation from the Holy Spirit on what my reaction should be. At one point, he asked me if I still wanted to pursue a relationship after knowing about his past. I kind of surprised myself by saying yes. When he asked me why, I told him, "Because I love you." Yes, I was the first one to say it.

God and Anger

The Bible talks about God's anger – His wrath being poured out on people and taking lives. But what most people don't understand about God's anger is that it's always birthed from a place of love.

> *"There are six things the Lord hates, seven that are detestable to him haughty eyes, a lying tongue, hands that shed innocent blood, a heart that devises wicked schemes, feet that are quick to rush into evil, a false witness who pours out lies, and a person who stirs up conflict in the community."*
> *Proverbs 6:16-19*

Whenever you see God's wrath poured out in scripture, you're sure to see that a group of people has done one or more of these things. When entire cities were annihilated it was because those people were involved in some horrific practices and teaching them to their children.

God's anger is always righteous. Ours tends to be self-righteous. We are "justified" in our anger. Our reactions to wrongs is "warranted." But God calls us to do better than that. He tells us:

> *"In your anger do not sin: Do not let the sun*

go down while you are still angry,"
Ephesians 4:26

We will get angry from time to time. The point is, what do we do with our anger... Something we will regret later, or something productive that will help the situation?

Warning Signs of Anger in a Relationship

We are going to get even more serious in the next two chapters. We're going to discuss warning signs for toxic relationships and abuse. It is extremely important that you understand what this looks like so that you can guard against getting into these kinds of relationships and be able to recognize the warning signs before things get serious.

Someone who gets angry easily is someone to stay away from. There are so many reasons why. A person who is easily angered needs time to work on themselves and get their anger and coping skills under control before they will be ready for a relationship.

Does he snap easily? If someone makes him angry, does he talk about harming that person or destroying their property? Is he quick to throw a punch if someone makes him mad? Does he get uncomfortably frustrated if you can't decide what movie you want to watch, or where you want to eat? Does he have road rage while driving? How does he handle disagreements or arguments in your relationship? Does he get angry to the point that all you want is for him to calm down or does it make you want to leave the situation or even fight back?

If a guy gets angry over stupid things occasionally, he may just be crabby, tired, or hungry. But, if dumb things set him off on a regular basis, he may have a real self-control or patience issue.

He may deal with self-doubt, low self-esteem, or mistrust. A guy like this needs a few more years to mature (hopefully) before he will be ready for a healthy relationship.

There are also more serious reasons for a man to not handle his anger correctly. He may have a mental health issue such as depression, anxiety, PTSD, or addiction. All of these are good reasons to stay away. He needs to be encouraged to get help to deal with these issues or he may not ever be ready to be in a mature relationship.

"How can I tell how serious his anger problem is?"

You can usually tell the difference between serious issues and non-serious issues by observation. First, if violence plays any role in his reactions, it's a huge red flag. If he's kindhearted and courteous 98% of the time, and only becomes disagreeable or snappy occasionally, give the guy a snickers. If that doesn't help, he may just need sleep, or to de-stress. If those don't bring back the prince charming you know and love, there may be underlying issues that can get worse later.

Let me make this abundantly clear…You cannot change or help someone with anger issues, depression, anxiety, PTSD, or any other mental disorder by getting into a relationship with them. Becoming emotionally connected and trying to "help" someone like this is bad for both of you. It won't help him, and it puts you into a dangerous situation. Let me repeat that. **It won't help him, and it puts you into a dangerous situation.**

Let's Talk About Abuse

First of all, remember this. Abuse happens everywhere. It doesn't matter how rich or poor someone is, how well educated someone is, where they live, what religion they claim, or what cultural or ethnic background they come from. Abuse comes from an evil nature. The evil nature comes from the devil's influence in the person's life. For the purpose of this book, I will be writing from the perspective that the woman is the victim, and the man is the abuser, but keep in mind, that women are also abused by women, and men are abused by other men and women as well.

"Why do people start abusing someone they claim to love?"

That really is the question, isn't it? I've put a lot of thought and research into why people do the things they do. Ultimately, there is no excuse, and the reasons are not good, but here's an attempt to understand where abuse comes from.

An abusive person may have been abused when they were young ... or even when they were older. Maybe they weren't abused directly, but maybe they witnessed abuse. Maybe they never learned how to relate to people in a healthy way. Maybe there is underlying anger from past trauma. Maybe they had everything taken away when they were younger, so they hold on to everything they have (including relationships) extremely tightly due to a subconscious fear that everything they have will be taken away again. Whatever the reason, abuse is never excusable, and you cannot fix an abuser. Only God can do that. But knowing the root cause can help you to recognize the potential for abuse in a relationship.

Please don't get me wrong ... past abuse or trauma does NOT mean that a victim is doomed to become an abuser. Many people become much better people than their abusers as a way to "rise above" their situation. The point is that the potential is there, so learn about the person's past. If there is something there, be watchful as you get to know that person better.

"How does a girl end up in an abusive relationship to begin with? Why would a girl want to be with a guy like this?"

No one daydreams about being in an abusive relationship. No one actively looks for a man that is mean and controlling. NO ONE wants to be abused. So, how do women get caught up in abusive relationships? Most of the time, it happens so slowly, or so quickly, she doesn't even realize it's happening until it's too late! Sometimes, she never realizes it. In these cases, it takes someone from the outside to point out to her all the signs of abuse before she will see it. Sometimes, that doesn't even help because she's so deep in denial that she refuses to believe it.

Most relationships that end up in abuse start out normally. They meet, they hit it off, things progress, and the relationship starts to get serious. Arguments start happening with more frequency. Something sets they guy off and he yells at her or hits her. They're both shocked, but the guy's pride wells up, and he starts blaming her for the abuse. "I'm sorry, but if you wouldn't have …" She is shaken but she loves him, so she accepts his apology on the hope that it won't happen again. But later on, it does happen again … and again … and again. Each time she doesn't stand up for herself, he feels that he is justified in doing it again in the future. The more often it happens the more she feels that it's deserved or normal.

Sometimes, she is caught up in drugs and ends up in a relationship with the guy that supplies the drugs for her. She is so addicted to the substance that she doesn't even see the abuse or doesn't care. On that note, sometimes she gets into a relationship with a "nice guy", and he is the one who introduces her to the drugs. (Side note: The use of drugs does not make the abuse her fault but is a possible side effect of making poor decisions)

Sometimes, she is so tired of waiting for "Mr. Right" that she settles for just any guy that is nice to her. He starts out their relationship by being kind and wanting to spend all of his time with her. He comes across as chivalrous and attentive ... She doesn't realize that under his jealousy and desire to always be together is a possessive and controlling spirit. Before long, he is telling her what to wear, where to go or not go, what friends she can have, and who she can or cannot talk to or hang out with.

There are many ways a person can end up in an abusive relationship, but the longer the abused allows the abuser to control her life, the more the abuser feels justified in abusing, and the harder it becomes for her to get out of the relationship.

In these situations, many of these men will apologize for their behavior. They will seem sincere and humble. They will promise that they will never do it again. Some of these men are so steeped in depression themselves that when they abuse, they feel like scum of the earth, so their apologies are sincere ... but that does not mean that it will not happen again. What it means is that this person needs professional help. Again, it also means that this person should not be in any kind of romantic relationship until they have learned how to deal with their own issues.

"Why doesn't she just leave?"

None of the reasons a woman will stay in an abusive relationship seem good enough. But their reasons for staying are just as real to them as your reasons for why they should leave. Many people have tried in vain to convince many victims to leave abusive relationships. Here are some of the reasons women have for staying:

1. The victim believes the abuse is her fault, and that if

she will just try harder, she can be the person he wants her to be, and their relationship will get better.
2. The victim believes she is the only one who can "fix" the abuser and he will become a better person.
3. The victim believes him every time he apologizes and promises to be better.
4. The victim has an unhealthy obsession with her abuser and won't leave him because she thinks she loves him.
5. The victim believes that she can take it, and if it's not her it will be someone else, and she doesn't wish that for someone else.
6. The victim believes she deserves the abuse.
7. The victim does not believe she deserves a better relationship.
8. The victim believes that this is normal – She doesn't realize that better relationships exist.
9. The victim believes that he will harm himself if she leaves and it will be her fault.
10. The victim believes that he will harm her or other people she loves if she leaves.
11. The victim feels stuck because she doesn't have friends, or family, she can turn to for help in getting out of this relationship. She is ashamed to ask for help or she doesn't want to be a burden to anyone.
12. The victim doesn't know about resources that are available to help her get out or doesn't think they will work.
13. The victim gets her drugs or alcohol supplied to her by her abuser.
14. The abuser keeps his victim too drunk or drugged to realize what's happening to her.
15. The victim feels that law enforcement won't believe her, and if she goes to them and tries to get them involved it will make matters worse, or that she will be in trouble with the law.

16. The victim has a false religious belief that she must remain in an abusive relationship because her religion commands it. (Speaking for followers of Jesus – God may hate divorce, but he also hates abuse. He commands us to love each other. Abuse is not love. There is no command to remain married to an abuser. A victim of abuse should get out. Period).
17. The idea of leaving him and starting a new life with absolutely nothing is absolutely terrifying for the victim.
18. The victim may not feel she has skills or experience to gain employment to support herself.
19. The abuser controls some or all the victim's assets, and she has no idea how to get control of them in order to start over.
20. If there are children involved, the victim may think that it's better for the children to have two parents in the home regardless of the abuse.
21. The victim may fear that the abuser will gain custody of the children or abuse them if she tries to leave.
22. The victim opens up to someone who doesn't believe them or the victim downplays it so much that the hearer doesn't take is seriously.

For most victims, leaving is extremely difficult. That is why it is important to get to know the person you're thinking of dating as well as you can. That way, if you notice red flags, you can avoid getting stuck in a situation like so many of these poor women. Most women who are stuck in abusive relationships will try to get out at least once. Even if she does get out, many of these women have been so messed up psychologically that they will return to their abuser. Studies have shown that if an abused woman doesn't get and stay out after several tries, she will either never get out, or she won't survive.

"How do I keep from getting into an abusive relationship?"

There is no 100% fool proof way of making sure you don't end up in an abusive relationship, but trusting your love life to God is a great place to start. If you let Him write your love story, He can lead you to someone who will love you the way God does. This gives you the best shot at a long and happy marriage as long as both you and your future husband keep God first in your lives.

We are going to discuss the warning signs of potential abuse so that you can avoid getting into a relationship with an abuser. If you are already in a relationship and start recognizing these signs, you can get out before you get "stuck" in a dangerous situation. If you do end up "stuck" in an abusive relationship before you realize it, there are steps you can take and people you can get a hold of to help you get out. We will discuss those more later.

"What does abuse look like?"

There are four basic types of abuse – Verbal, Psychological, Physical, and Sexual. Most people caught up in abuse are caught up in two or more of them. Verbal abuse goes hand in hand with psychological abuse with only a few differences. Physical abuse is usually accompanied by verbal abuse. Even though Physical abuse is not always Sexual abuse, Sexual abuse is always Physical abuse. Basically, abuse is a tangled web, and every type is detrimental.

There are some general characteristics to watch out for as red flags for potential abusers. A potential abuser may:

1. Be the jealous type. He won't like it when his girlfriend is talking with other guys. He tends to get hurt or angry when she wants to spend time with her girlfriends.

2. Become sulky and silent when upset.
3. Have an explosive temper. If he has road rage or gets rude with a waiter for getting his order wrong. Be watchful.
4. Criticize and put down others (ither jokingly or seriously), is not a good sign.
5. Have difficulty expressing his own feelings.
6. Drink heavily or use drugs.
7. Show disrespect for people in general, or specifically women.
8. Be overly or obsessively "protective".
9. Minimize or deny blame – shift responsibility for his actions to anyone or anything but himself. He denies that he is abusing because his actions are not his own fault.
10. Have been abused as a child or witnessed abuse - Many abusive men have a history of exposure to abuse when they were young.
11. Want to know every detail of the time the victim spends away from them and may try to find inconsistencies in the victim's story in order to punish the victim later.
12. Will compare the victim to an ex and/or complain about their ex, blaming their ex for the failed relationship.

Verbal Abuse

Verbal abuse is the use of words to intimidate, cut down the victim, express anger to the victim, and to keep the victim compliant to the abuser's wishes. It is marked by anger. Usually, a verbal abuser is simply misdirecting inward anger upon his victim. He has issues from his past that have not been dealt with, and he doesn't have any healthy outlet to keep his anger under control. The people closest to someone like this get the brunt of his outbursts.

Someone prone to verbal abuse may:

1. Have difficulty communicating. When pressed to discuss certain things, he may become angry, dismissive, or change the subject in such a way that the victim gets the impression that it is not wise to bring it up again.
2. Tell rude jokes about his victim. The abuser may even claim that he is only joking, but the words will still sting, and the victim will usually know that the joke was said specifically to be mean.
3. Has to win every argument. In its beginning stages, the need to win arguments may seem like no big deal, even comical. But, if someone just can't ever admit when he is wrong, it's a red flag.
4. Find it fun to humiliate his victim. The abuser tells embarrassing stories about the victim in an effort to make her feel small. He may also make her feel stupid for her opinions.
5. Be condescending. When someone talks down to people, he is trying to feel superior or powerful. In a relationship, he may treat his victim like a child making himself the "authority" in the relationship.
6. Look for things to blame the victim for. He needs to be angry about something, so he will pick fights with his girlfriend over the stupidest of things. "You made me miss my turn," "That's my pen, why are you using it?" "Why were you talking to that guy?" "Your friends don't like me. You shouldn't be friends with them." "You do everything your mom tells you to do, don't you?" "Why didn't you text me back?"
7. Call people mean and hurtful names. First off, name calling is never ok. But an abuser is excessive in the name calling department. It may start out as joking,

but over time, can turn into a nasty and horrible way to cut down his victim.
8. Criticize or demean the victim. An abuser will criticize his victim for almost any stupid thing. He might criticize her for what friends she has, what her hobbies are, how she talks, or what she wants to do with her life after High School. He may say things like, "You'd be more attractive if…" "That looks stupid on you." "You're fat." "You're stupid." "You're too sensitive."
9. Yell or raise his voice. Yelling is meant to get people's attention, sound alarms, cheer people on at games, or to celebrate things. And yes, we've all yelled out of anger from time to time. But an abuser tends to use yelling as a default to get his point across. Yelling should never be used to cut someone down or take away their dignity.

Psychological Abuse

Psychological abuse capitalizes on the emotions of the victim to make the victim feel like less of a person, or that they need to become someone else to please their abuser. A psychological abuser has a need to control or change the victim. Usually, this kind of abuse is brought on by trauma in the past. The abuser has likely gone through things he cannot control, so he has learned how to manipulate and control situations and people around him in an attempt to make his ideal world or relationship.

Here are some examples and characteristics that are more specific to psychological abuse. Someone who is psychologically abusive may:

1. Manipulate his victim. An abuser will manipulate situations in their own favor. As long as he gets what he wants, he doesn't care if he hurts or inconveniences

her. "If you hadn't…than I wouldn't have…" "If you would just…, then I would…" "If you really loved me you would…" "I'm just going to leave you. Then where will you be?" "I would love you more if you would…" "But I did … for you. You could show some appreciation." "If you really trusted me, you would give me your passwords." (Ladies, DO NOT give out ANY of your passwords until you are in a trusted marriage relationship).
2. Be dismissive of the victim's feelings. He may be driving too fast, and she says something about it. He dismisses her fear and tells her she's fine. She may be upset over the loss of a friendship. He tells her that it's no big deal and to let it go.
3. Tell his victim how she should feel. She tells him that he hurt her feelings and he tells her not to make a big deal about it. "Lighten up." "You're such a crybaby."
4. Devalue his victim. He makes the victim feel that she has no say, or that what she has to say is not important.
5. Undermines her decisions. She is trying to do something, and he takes it from her to do himself as if she can't do it. She makes a decision to do something, and he makes it impossible for her to do, or changes the situation so that what he wants takes place instead.
6. Won't let things go. Long after the argument is over, an abuser will keep bringing up all the things he feels the victim did wrong. This way, she will always feel guilty and like she has to "make up" for her wrongdoings.
7. Control his partner's behavior, money, and decisions. The abuser tells the victim what to do on a consistent basis. "Why didn't you ask me first?" "Go get me …" "You can't go there…" "You can't do that…" "Don't talk to him." "You can't hang out with them anymore." He treats his partner almost as if she is a servant or a child.
8. Blames the victim for things the victim has little or no control over. Losing a job, being denied a job, missing

out on an event, not being able to purchase something, or almost anything the abuser wants to place blame for.

9. Use intimidation to take away her power. He may use looks, actions, gestures, or tones of voice to criticize, cut down, manipulate, or scare his victim. If that doesn't work, he may smash things, destroy property, abuse pets, and/or display weapons to show his victim that he means business and is not to be crossed.

10. Isolation/Exclusion. Psychological abusers want to keep their victims close and isolated from their friends and family. He may control what she reads, what she watches on TV, or where she goes and who she talks to. He limits her outside involvement using jealousy to justify his actions. "I just want to spend all of my time with you." "You don't need to worry about what's going on out there. We are all that matters."

11. Gaslight his victim. During an argument, an abuser will twist the story with such conviction that the victim will start to question if they remembered the situation correctly. This puts the victim on shaky ground and makes the argument easy for the abuser to win…even when he is in the wrong. In addition, an abuser can twist and misshape reality so that the victim no longer sees the world around her as a safe place to be. When he uses these mind games, she may begin to mistrust her family and friends because of the lies he feeds her. She will then become dependent only upon her abuser. "People don't really like you. You should hear what they say behind your back." "Your parents don't really care about you. If they did, they would let you…"

12. Define the roles each person should play in a relationship. "I'm the man, so you have to do as I say." "You're the woman so you're supposed to…"

13. Threaten his victim. If he does not get what he wants,

and manipulation isn't working, an abuser may resort to threats. He can threaten some kind of harm to her, her kids, or her family, or it may be something as little as withholding something from her until he gets what he wants. He may also use fear tactics to keep her silent about the abuse she's going through. He may threaten to expose her weaknesses or spread rumors about her to her peers or over social media if she says anything. If she tries to leave the relationship, he may threaten to harm himself or commit suicide. This throws her into an emotional rollercoaster. She wants to leave, but she doesn't want to feel responsible for him injuring or killing himself.
14. Dictate what his victim can wear or how much she can weigh in order to be acceptable to him.

With both verbal and psychological abuse, sometimes the abuser realizes he's doing it, but sometimes he doesn't. The abuser justifies his actions because no one was physically hurt. He is under the false impression that emotional damage is not as bad as physical damage.

Ok. Take a deep breath. I know that was a lot to go through. We still have to talk about physical and sexual abuse, so take a breather before diving into the next chapter.

Love Does Not Delight in Evil

Chapter 11

Noun: 'profound immorality, wickedness, and depravity, especially when regarded as a supernatural force.'

My Story

Over the next couple of months, our relationship grew quickly. Because we both lived up in the mountains and a decent drive away from civilization, we spent a lot of time together. He was still working on my parent's house and helped finish the loft in the garage so that I could move in there and have my own space. We were not really "alone" much as my parents were usually home or we were over at his parent's house having dinner or something, but the speed of progression of the relationship and how close I was feeling to him so quickly kind of scared me. Plus, the information about his past was still kind of fresh and I needed some time to process it. So, I told him that I needed to slow down our relationship a bit. We spent a little less time together while I took a breath and processed what was happening with my life. But...

On November 10th, 2006, Frankie took me on my first "official" date to a cute little Basque restaurant. We dressed up and had a wonderful time. Shortly afterward, I put our relationship on hold for a little while. Even though we decided that we both wanted to move forward in this relationship, and were working toward marriage, I was nervous and cautious. The newness of this relationship and how fast I was bonding with him had me on guard. I was still trying to process the information about his past and decide if the effects of it were something I could live with for the rest of my life. This was serious and I knew it. I had never been in a relationship before. I had so carefully guarded my heart for many years. Was this really happening? Frankie was not easily discouraged by my hesitation. He kept gently pursuing me and melted me down with his love for God, his kind and respectful nature, and with that goofy grin of his.

On Valentines Day 2007, Frankie took me out for a Valentines dinner and gave me a promise ring. It was similar to the purity ring I was wearing, but it had 3 hearts on it, whereas mine only had one. He told me that the two little hearts were me and him, and the big heart in the middle was God. I was honored and embarrassed because I had just gotten him a little plaque with a scripture on it. Not to mention, other people at the restaurant thought he was proposing to me.

A promise ring! I had a boyfriend and a promise that his intentions were to work with me toward marriage. I was on cloud nine.

God Hates Evil

I hope we can all agree that abuse in any form is evil. Satan has taken every good and perfect gift that God has given us and found a way to mutilate it and turn it into something wrong and ugly. When it comes to abuse, he uses fear to keep God's children under his thumb. He knows that each and every girl that God created can be a force to reckon with. If he can keep her under his control, she won't be able to realize her true potential. She won't understand that God has created her for great things.

There is so much evil in this world. Satan has corrupted the world to the point that most people only think of themselves and what can satisfy them. They don't mind doing evil things as long as they think it will satisfy some desire of theirs.

God hates evil. But He loves us. If we turn to Him, He can wash all the evil of the world off of us and create for us a pure heart and a new life. A life that avoids evil at all costs because we understand God's great love for us and His good plan for our lives. We learn to do good because His good nature is growing inside of us and we want to please Him. If not for the changing power of God, I would not have trusted that Frankie had changed from his old life.

Evil in Relationships

The reason I categorized Physical and Sexual abuse under "Love does not delight in Evil" is because both kinds of abuse are so blatant that the abuser absolutely knows that he is hurting someone. He can try to deny it to himself, but no matter what, he knows what he is doing is dead wrong. He is under the influence and/or control of Satan's minions at this point.

"If he knows it's wrong, why does he do it?"

Ultimately, it has to do with pride and power. As much as a woman wants to be loved and cherished, a man wants to be respected. When both roles are played properly, a beautiful and healthy relationship can result. However, when a man demands respect instead of earning it, he starts skating on a thin line between simply being rude and a controlling type of abuse. If a woman stands up to him, she risks being hurt, but if she doesn't, she's being controlled which is equally as dangerous.

Now, let's talk about physical and sexual abuse in more detail. This is going to be intense, and some of it may be hard to swallow, but this is very important information to have. You need to be armed with the knowledge of exactly where these types of abuse come from and what they look like. This way you can stay away from guys that exhibit the warning signs or find the help you need if you find yourself caught up in an abusive relationship.

Physical Abuse

While there are many ways someone may become an abuser, I'd like to give a play-by-play example of the process someone can go through to become a particularly heinous abuser. When a girl gets into a relationship with an abuser, she may be stepping into the beginning or middle of the process, or she may meet the guy after he's been at the abusing game for a while.

There are a few factors to consider as to why an abuser may start abusing. Perhaps he was raised by abusers and thinks it's normal. Perhaps he has lost control of things in his life, and it makes him so angry that he feels he needs to lash out. Perhaps he has some kind of mental issue that requires professional help. Whatever the reason, it's best to stay away or get away from someone like this, no matter how much you like him or think you can help him.

Power can be very addictive. One of the reasons for an abuser to start abusing may have to do with addiction to power. As an abusive man gains power in a relationship, he starts getting a "high" of sorts from the adrenaline that is released when he gets emotionally charged. This is called "anger addiction." When the "high" wears off, he might feel bad for what he did, but his pride won't allow him to admit he was wrong and change. Instead, life goes on until he finds another reason to get angry or controlling. As the next "high" sets in, he again loses his sense of common decency and respect for the girl until the high wears off again. Around and around he goes. But, like any addiction, the more "highs" he experiences, the more he wants them. The more he wants them, the more often he will look for reasons to get "high" again. He will start to nitpick at any stupid thing to get angry. Then the hitting or sexual abuse starts. Yelling or manipulating aren't enough anymore. His body has grown accustomed to the adrenaline, and he needs something more intense in order to get "high." Hitting and sexual abuse both cause bursts of adrenaline, so they are a natural next step.

Most of the signs for a verbal abuser and a psychological abuser will be the same for a physical abuser, especially since physical abuse is usually a "next step" after verbal or psychological abuse. The only notable difference between the signs for psychological abuse and physical abuse have to do with follow through. A psychological abuser may just threaten to do something damaging, whereas a physical abuser will follow through with the threat.

When it comes to keeping yourself safe, watch out for all the signs of an abuser, but pay close attention to the signs that have the most violent potential, like threats of harm, and destruction of property.

Sexual Abuse

Let me pause here. While most people understand that forcing someone to have sex against their will is rape, not everyone recognizes where that line is drawn. So, let's spell it out.
1. The definition of rape as stated by the United States Department of Justice is "the penetration, no matter how slight, of the vagina or anus with any body part or object, or oral penetration by a sex organ of another person, without the consent of the victim." The Arizona Collation to end sexual & domestic Violence states, "Rape is any unwanted sexual contact obtained without consent through the use of force, threat of force, intimidation, or coercion.

2. Rape is not just committed by someone who does not know their victim. In fact, most victims know their attacker.
3. Being snatched off the street and forced to have sex – is Rape.
4. Being forced to have sex during a date – is Rape.
5. Being pressured into having sex during a date – is Rape.
6. Being intimidated into having sex – is Rape.
7. Being forced to have sex even though you are married – is Rape.
8. Being forced to orally please someone – is rape.
9. Having sex while being on drugs or drunk to the point of not being able to give coherent consent – is rape.

Here are also a few misconceptions that need to be cleared up:

1. Just because the victim did not put up a fight does not mean that it wasn't rape.
2. A person is not "asking to be raped" by their actions or they way they dress.
3. It is not just women who are raped. Men and boys have also been raped by other men or women.
4. Just because the victim became "aroused" during the attack does not mean it wasn't rape.
5. "No" means "No"
6. Not giving a "Yes" also means "No"
7. Giving a "Yes" only because of intimidation, pressure, or coercion might be harder to convict, but if the victim didn't want it, it's still rape and is still emotionally damaging.

"But, he says if I love him I'll have sex with him."

Ladies, this is called sexual coercion. Men who sexually abuse their victims manipulate situations in order to get sex.

1. They make sexual and inappropriate jokes
2. They tend to be very "handsy." He might grab her butt, "accidentally" grab her breasts, tickle and tease her inappropriately. His hands may go under her clothes and then tell her that he's just "messing around." Most girls that feel uncomfortable with these advances are too shy or feel too awkward to push back and tell him to stop. But, if she doesn't learn to stand up for herself, he will continue to make her feel uncomfortable, and is more likely to push her into having sex when she doesn't want to.
3. They might make threats or get their victims drunk or drugged in order to get them to comply with their wishes.
4. Some will even get a girl pregnant on purpose in order to use the pregnancy or child to keep her locked into a relationship with him. ... "For the sake of the child."

The sexual drive in men is generally much higher than it is in women. Because of this, guys who have not learned self-control have a very difficult time accepting "no" for an answer. They will do almost anything to get sex from you. Begging, manipulating, forcing...For a guy who has not learned the value of relationships, the value of women, and the value of saving sex for marriage, almost nothing is off the table. And, if you don't give it up, he will typically either find other ways to "get off," or he will leave you for someone who will satisfy his sexual desires. Either way, this is not the kind of guy you want to be in a relationship with.

So, if a guy keeps pushing you for sex, or sexual favors, my recommendation is to get out as quickly as you can. It's not fair to you to constantly be pushed to do things you are not comfortable with. It is not fair to him to keep him in a relationship that is not going to give him what he wants. Let him go, and hopefully someday he will mature enough to understand the real meaning of love and be respectful and faithful to the next girl.

Now that we've discussed the different types of abuse, let's talk about what to do if you suspect that one of your friends is being abused.

In addition to watching that you don't end up in an abusive relationship, it is also very important to watch out for your friends. If you see something that causes you to be concern about their relationship, SPEAK UP! It's better to offend your friend or let her have a broken heart because of the breakup than for her to end up or stay in an abusive relationship. You also have the power to speak up if you see abuse happening to a complete stranger. Call the police, call for security, call friends to come help, but don't be afraid to make a stand against abuse.

"How do I know for sure, and what should I do about it?"

First off, pray. God loves your friend very much and doesn't want her to be in an abusive relationship. If there is anyone who can help you figure out if she is being abused and what to do about it, it is Him. Second, watch how they interact with each other and other people. There are many signs that abusers and victims will display to the outside world which will shine a light into what is happening behind closed doors.

Here are some characteristics of an abusive relationship to watch for. If one or two of the "less scary" things pop up in the relationship every once in a while, that is not necessarily cause for concern, but if you are seeing things happen frequently, be on guard and start asking questions.

An abused woman may:

1. Show fear about how her partner may react to a situation
2. Often comply to her partner's wishes because she doesn't want to hurt his feelings or upset him
3. Frequently break dates with "the girls" to be with her boyfriend
4. Become withdrawn under stress
5. Have the urge to "rescue" her partner when he is troubled
6. Talk about her partner in an almost obsessive manner
7. Frequently apologize for her partner's behavior
8. Slip up and mention something about the abuse but downplay it or write it off as an accident.
9. Have an unusually strong belief in traditional male/female roles (He is head of the house, and I'm supposed to serve him)
10. Often make decisions about activities and friends according to what her partner wants or how her partner would react regardless of her own opinion
11. Show signs of physical abuse such as an unusually high number of wounds, bruising, or scars, but have an ambiguous story or reason for each one. She will usually attempt to hide her wounds with clothing, accessories, hairstyle, or makeup and claim that she's "such a klutz."
12. Have been abused as a child or witnessed abuse – Many women who end up in abusive relationships have a history of exposure to abuse when they were young

Since each of the partners in an abusive relationship feels inadequate and incomplete, they tend to look to the relationship to feel "complete." It is as if they two together form a "whole" person. Thus, the relationship is often a symbolic one: the partners feel unable to exist without each other. This extreme mutual dependency makes separation very difficult for both partners.

For this reason, helping a friend who is in an abusive relationship is an extremely hard thing to do. Many of these women, even if you convince them that they are being abused, simply won't leave. But that doesn't mean you shouldn't try. Use the information you will learn in this book to expose abuse and to explain what love is. Hopefully, she will understand and want to get out of the relationship herself. If she is under 18, get in touch with a trusted adult who has the power to do something about this dangerous situation. If you witness abuse in any form, report it. It is better for your friend to be mad at you than for you to leave her in a dangerous situation.

After doing everything you can do to help your friend, there may come a point at which there is nothing else you can do. In those cases, continue to pray for her, and let her know you will always be there for her if she wants or needs you. Then, let her go. Rest assured, God will continue to work on the situation.

> ***"If I find myself or a friend stuck in an abusive relationship, where can I get help?"***

If there is immediate danger, please get a hold of the police. There are a lot of bad reports about the police going around the media and social media. I understand the thought of going to the police can be scary. But there are a lot of really good police as well. Many are good people who used to be kids that wanted to grow up to put on a badge and help people. If going to the police is just too intimidating, head to a fire station or a hospital. They are there to help. At least give it a try.

If you or your friend is scared of getting caught by the abuser, find a Family Resource Center and make an anonymous visit. They know how to find people specifically trained in how to help.

If you have access to internet, google, "how to get out of an abusive relationship." There will be organizations that pop right up to the top of the search with phone numbers you can call for help. If you need access to the internet, utilize your local library. All you need is a library card, and you can have access to the internet for free.

Find a school and talk to a teacher or office worker. Or find a church and talk to a pastor. They have resources and phone numbers to call to keep you safe and get you out of the situation.

Whatever you do, don't just sit back and take it. You deserve better. You're worth more. God created you for great things. Don't let the devil take away your value for any reason, but especially don't let him take it away because of some idiot guy who claims to "love" you one minute and hurts you the next.

Love Rejoices With the Truth

Chapter 12

Noun: 'That which is true or in accordance with fact or reality.'

My Story

When I met Frankie, there was much to learn about him and his past. As I learned about it, I had to come to terms with the fact that the natural consequences of his past would be something we would have to work with together if we were to be married. I had to decide if I was going to trust that this man that I was just getting to know would not return to the lifestyle he had come out of.

I spent many days and even months bringing this subject before God. Could I trust that this man would be faithful to God and to our vows if we marry? Could I trust that he would not return to the lifestyle he had come out of? Then, God started doing something amazing.

One of my favorite places to talk to God was in the car. Because of where I lived, it took time to get just about anywhere. This gave me plenty of opportunity to think and pray. I used this time to pour out my heart to God and discuss all of my concerns about the future. Every time I brought up Frankie's past with God, a song would come on the radio. The song is called "I'm not who I was," by Brandon Heath. I swear, it happened so often that as the song came on I would shake my head and smile.

"Ok, ok. I get it. He's not who he used to be."

This was my promise from God that He truly had stepped into Frankie's life and made it completely new. Frankie was not the man with the dark past anymore. He was the man with the bright future. My only job was to trust that the God I serve was faithful and strong enough to make that complete of a change in someone.

God is Truth

> *"Jesus Answered, 'I am the way, and the truth, and the life. No one comes to the Father except through me.'"*
> *John 14:6*

Jesus was perfect. He never sinned, which means He also never lied. If you truly read the Bible in context, you can easily see that everything Jesus said was backed up by His actions. He taught His disciples to be truthful and wise. His Holy Spirit was sent to us to teach us truth after Jesus left Earth.

If you are a child of God, you should be reading His Word. If you read His Word, the promise is that you will be able to discern truth from lie in this world.

> *"...If you hold to my teaching, you are really my disciples. Then you will know the truth, and the truth will set you free."*
> *John 8:32*

The world tells us to "live our truth." But, if our truth doesn't line up with the Word of God, there is something deep inside us that knows and understands that "our truth" is actually a lie. If we live "our truth" we are actually just putting a shiny mask over His Truth. This will leave us always searching out new ways to "live our truth," because we will be left with a deep sense of dissatisfaction.

We need to peel the mask of "our truth" off our faces and ask God to show us HIS Truth in our lives. Only then will we find truth joy and contentment.

Truth in Relationships

Ah, the truth. Why is the truth something that people don't take seriously unless someone lies to them? "It's ok for me to lie to you, but it's not ok for you to lie to me." Personally, I pride myself on telling the truth in all circumstances, but I will admit that if I don't think the truth is going to be well received, I still want to put my own spin on it to make it more palatable. "Yes, we're heading out now." Really means, "I'm TRYING to get out the door, but the kids still haven't gotten their shoes on." I'm not exactly lying, but I am being ambiguous enough that the listener gets the impression that I have it all under control and am on my way. But, when my husband is locking up at work, I want to know the details. "So, does 'leaving now' mean that the doors are locked and you're in your truck?" If we're honest, we give ourselves a lot more grace than we do others.

What if we raised our standards? What if we demanded truth from ourselves as much as we do others? What would happen to the world around us? Honestly, I don't know, but I think it would be interesting to see.

"How do I become a truthful person?"

First: Be true to yourself. You may or may not have a good idea of who you are at this point in your life, but you can draw from things you do know. Do you like guacamole? If the answer is "yes," stand on it! If the answer is "no," don't let anyone pressure you into putting guacamole on your tacos. Are you scared to try drugs, but your friends are pressuring you? Stand up for yourself. You already know that's not who you want to be, so walk away. Make new friends who will support a positive and healthy life.

Second: Be true to God's calling on your life. If you don't know what that is, yet that's totally ok! Maybe you are just starting to realize that God loves you and never realized that He's got some good stuff that he's ready to do in your life. Spend time getting to know Him. Read your Bible. If you don't have one, ask a church to give you one. Hang around other people who know Him. If you do, His promise is that you will find Him and that you will find truth.

> *"If you seek me you will find me, if you seek me with all your heart."*
> *Jeremiah 29:13*

Third: Be true to your relationship standards. Seriously. We're talking about the person you're going to be the closest to and the most vulnerable with. You're going to be opening up the deepest parts of who you are with another human being. Be careful! Set ridiculously high (but realistic) standards. Then, stick to them. It doesn't even matter if your friends think your standards are too high. Set your standards so high, only one will rise to meet them.

If you truly believe that God has the best plan for your life, let Him guide you while you're setting your standards. Spend some time praying about what you're looking for in a man. Open your heart to His whispers describing the kind of man you can spend the rest of your life with. Write down what you're feeling. You'll be glad you did.

"Aren't 'white lies' ok?"

First off, lying is still lying no matter how big or small it is or who you lie to. It breaks trust between you and the person who you're lying to. Lying to your parents or teachers will more likely get you into trouble than it will get you out of trouble. And even if you do manage to get away with lying to them, remember that God knows all about it. Your lies will find a way to come back around and bite you. God loves you too much to let you keep lying, so there will be consequences. Either your lie will find you out, you'll have to lie to cover lies until the whole thing crumbles down, someone will lie to you, or you'll be eaten alive by the guilt until you come clean. God is a very creative God. He knows what's going to get through to you. So, remember, it's just better to be honest from the beginning.

> *"If you always tell the truth, you don't have to remember anything."* — Author - unknown

Be truthful, but tactful. I have said this over and over again, "It's not what you say, but how you say it." Some people pride themselves on being brutally honest. They don't really care if they hurt someone because they were, "...just being honest. If they can't handle the truth, that's not my fault." There's a difference between being an honest person and just using the truth to bully someone. "If you can't say anything nice, don't say anything at all" applies in this case. If you need to say something, and you want to be honest, for goodness sake, find a way to be tactful. If someone asks you if you like their outfit but you really don't, either find something about it you can like, or you can just say "It's not my style, but that's ok! I'm glad you like it." Most of the time, there'll be something you can say about the color. "It matches your hair," "it brings out your eyes," or "it's a good color on you" will work.

Most people find it easier to be truthful with their friends than with just about anyone. They'll lie to their family, teachers, or even their boyfriend, but are totally honest with their friends. But occasionally, a subject might come up that you just don't want to be honest about. If there's something you really just don't want to talk about, "I really just don't want to talk about it." Is a completely legitimate answer.

That said, if something has gone horribly wrong in your life, and you feel unsafe, and you are uncomfortable going to an adult with it, find a trusted friend to confide in. If it's something serious and an adult should get involved, you can ask your friend to help you figure out who to go to for help. Please don't lie to yourself that you can handle it on your own, or that it will all just go away. God made us to need each other. It's ok to find someone to help you.

"How important is truthfulness in a relationship?"

There are people who will say that you do not have to be totally truthful in a relationship. For instance, these people say it is unwise to tell your significant other about past relationships. They argue that what's in the past is in the past, and it shouldn't matter to your current relationship. This couldn't be further from the truth! Your past might be "in the past" but it has shaped who you are now. Also, there is always a chance of running into an old boyfriend at some point in your life. That can make things awkward to begin with, but if your current boyfriend or husband doesn't know about him, imagine what would happen if he found out? Or, think about it the other way around. If your man ran into an old fling, how would you feel if he didn't mention anything about it. I can imagine it would even be awkward if he introduced someone to you as an old girlfriend... that you never knew about.

You've seen the movies. The guy is going about his business. Some girl comes along and flirts with him. A kiss happens. Sometimes it's his fault, sometimes hers, sometimes mutual, but the fact is, it happened. The problem is that the guy isn't single. The guy decides for one reason or another to not tell his girlfriend or wife. You want to throw a pillow at the screen because he's being stupid, and she's going to find out anyway. Sure enough, she finds out, and it doesn't go well.

Yes, the movies are just acting, and it's all dramatic, but there is truth in this one. Don't hide things like this from your significant other! If someone flirts with you, tell him. If another guy makes you uncomfortable, tell him. If you find yourself caught in a compromising situation and a kiss happens, tell him. If you want out of the relationship because of it, just get it over with! If he wants out of the relationship because he suddenly doesn't trust you anymore, it's because he wasn't completely sold on the relationship to begin with! If you both can get past it and move on, fabulous! But if you hide it, it won't end well. Either he'll find out, or you'll mull it over and over in your head until it drives you crazy.

Some people will hide past relationships because it was a bad experience they don't want to relive. Maybe they're uncomfortable discussing how far the relationship went physically. There are also instances where the person hasn't really let the person go and are keeping their options open. The fact is, none of these are good reasons to hold back the information. If you truly love the person you're in a relationship with, you should be able to trust them with all of that information... except for the last one. If someone hides a previous relationship because they still have feelings for the person and secretly hope to get back together with them, they need to end their current relationship and figure that out for themselves.

Openness and honesty are key to a healthy and long-lasting relationship. If you're getting serious about someone, sit down with him and have the talk about the past. Have a calm and rational discussion about it. Do not be over emotional or defensive about the conversation. Take a breath if you feel your emotions welling up and getting away from you. Ask God for patience and wisdom. Discuss how many previous relationships there were, how involved you were with that person, how far you went physically, how you feel about that person now, and what lessons you learned from that relationship. Your current relationship should become stronger from the honesty. And if you find out things about him that are just too much to handle, or visa versa, you'll be glad that it all came out now and not after you were more emotionally invested in this guy.

Be truthful about your feelings. Please, oh please, don't bottle up your feelings for the sake of any relationship. It will destroy you and your relationship from the inside out. Be honest with him if he has hurt your feelings, if you've had a bad day, if you're hormonal, if that movie brought up some bad memories, or anything else that may come up. Share with him your victories, the good days, the friend you hadn't seen in forever, the things you're learning, or how much you love him and why. You will learn more about each other, and how to care for each other in a deeper way. Or you will discover that you are not compatible and need to reevaluate the relationship before anyone gets hurt. Either way, being open and honest will protect you both.

Don't trust a guy who is willing to lie to his parents to get what he wants. He will do the same to you. No, you're not different because you're his girlfriend. If he's willing to lie to his parents, he will be willing to lie to you. Even if he doesn't do it while you're dating, after you get married, he will settle into "family mode" and the lies will start. You can believe me or not, but I can tell you that it's true. How a man treats his family is one of the biggest indications of how he will treat his wife. If you would not like to be treated the way he treats his family, get out of the relationship, because it will happen if you stay.

Even "white lies" don't belong in your relationship. They set a standard that it's ok to be dishonest with your significant other. Like many other compromises, if you start doing it, not only will it keep happening, but it will get worse over time until the "white lies" have turned into "big lies," the kind that put the relationship in jeopardy. If you lie to each other even in the little things, it breeds mistrust in the big things. "If he's willing to lie about this, what else is he willing to lie about?" Make honesty one of your "must haves" for your relationship. Accept nothing less.

Here's Some Truth for You

"For God so loved the world that He gave is one and only son, that whoever believes in Him should not die, but have everlasting life. For God did not send His son into the world to condemn the world but to save the world through Him."
John 3:16-17

God is saying, "I'm laying it all out there, guys. I love you so much that I was willing to send my only son to take on the punishment for all the things that you did wrong. I know you deserve the punishment of death for your own mistakes. I don't care. I love you too much to let that be the end of the story. So, I'm going to take all of that guilt, place it on myself, and take on the punishment. All you have to do is believe with all your heart that

I've done this. Come to me, and I will wash all your sins away and give you new life."

The truth is, there's a God who loves you and created you perfectly with your personality, your eye color, your hair type, your skin tone, your height, and your body type. He created you for a purpose. He has a plan for your life which will impact the world around you. He gave you certain gifts and talents to cultivate and use to do amazing things in the world. Then, He gave you a choice. You can love and accept who you are and who He has created you to be, or you can give it all up and walk away. He's not going to force you to do anything you don't want to do or be anything you don't want to be. The choice is yours.

> "'For I know the plans I have for you,' declares the Lord. 'Plans to prosper you and not to harm you. Plans to give you a hope and a future.'"
> Jeremiah 29:11

Weather you accept it or not, God has great plans for you. He won't force you to follow His plans, but if you allow Him to, He can use you for amazing things. I can promise that if you fully surrender to Him, and take on His plan for your life, you won't regret it. That's the truth. Take it or leave it.

Love Always Protects

Chapter 13

Verb: 'To keep safe from harm or injury.'

My Story

Frankie and I spent the next several months getting to know each other, spending time together, getting to know each other's families, and talking about the life we were preparing to start together. At one point, we went ring shopping, and I picked out the most beautiful wedding ring I had fallen in love with. Frankie put a down payment on it and started saving up to pay it off.

I wish I could say that everything was carefree and wonderful during this time, but due to some unforeseen circumstances, my dad decided that he wasn't as on-board with us getting married as he had originally thought. He wanted us to wait. I struggled with what to do with this information. I didn't want to dishonor my dad, but I felt that God had sent this man to me and had given my heart the ok to get married. Everyone had an opinion, and my mind was in turmoil while it was being pulled so many different directions. I decided to take 3 days to fast and pray. I locked myself away from everyone, including Frankie.

At the end of the three days, Frankie picked me up for a surprise picnic on the top of a mountain during the sunset. He brought up some devotional books which he read to me, and then, as it was getting dark, he asked me to marry him. For months, he had asked me, on a nearly daily basis, but I told him I wouldn't answer the question until he had a ring. He asked me, I told him that he knew I wouldn't answer the question, and then he pulled himself up onto one knee, pulled the ring out, and said, "now will you answer me?" Of course, I said, "Yes!"

The next year of our lives was hard. We were engaged, but because of my dad, we did not set a date. We worked through some stresses and problems; we had many times alone which ended badly because we were getting too close physically. Even though we never had sex, and didn't even kiss, we did cross a few lines I hadn't realized were lines to cross. We got too comfortable, and hands wandered a little too much. We didn't kiss on the mouth, but I hadn't realized that kissing on the neck could raise so many feelings.

Because of these stresses, we broke up several times. These times crushed me because I knew Frankie was the man I wanted to marry, but what I didn't understand was that he really needed those breaks in order to honor the commitment we had both made to wait until our wedding day to have sex. He was protecting me. He was protecting himself. He was protecting our relationship before God in the best way he could think of at the time.

God's Protection

God loves you with an everlasting love. He proved it when he died to protect you from the guilt of your own sins. He is the ultimate example of protection in your life. Without Him, you wouldn't breathe. He has likely saved you from being hurt or killed on countless occasions, but you'll never know about it because He did it by setting things in motion that were completely out of your control.

That trip you didn't get to go on? Maybe there was going to be a drunk driver on the road. That person that stopped you to talk? Maybe there was someone ahead you would have run into that would have mugged you. That boy who shattered your heart by dumping you right before prom? Maybe he was going to be an abusive husband. We'll never know for sure, but I do believe that God cares for us enough to do things like this.

Protect Yourself

Let's talk about your own protection. If you don't care enough to protect yourself, you're going to end up doing things you regret, or getting into situations that are hard to get out of. If you protect yourself, you may still end up doing things you regret, or getting into situations that are hard to get out of, but your chances are better, and those things are likely to not be as bad.

Be smart. Use the information you've found in this book as tools and guidelines to keep yourself as far away from dangerous situations as possible. Travel with trusted friends. Never go on blind dates or dates with someone you just met without an exit strategy, backup plan, and someone who knows where you are and what you're doing. Don't let him pick you up or know where you live. Keep yourself close to people who can help you and pay attention to any warning signs. There should always be someone somewhere nearby who can help you if you need to get out of an uncomfortable situation, even if it's a server at a restaurant. After all, you are getting to know each other, but you don't necessarily know him that well yet. You may even get to the restaurant early and ask your server to keep an eye on you because you don't know this guy very well, and you just want to make sure you have a backup if needed.

It is very important to be careful about where you spend your time, and who you spend it with. Raves, clubs, party houses, and many regular teen hangouts can be very dangerous. Drunk and high people are unpredictable. Fights break out, people hallucinate and do dangerous and scary things. Predators hang around places like this looking for easy targets. People disappear from places like this.

Never ever walk anywhere alone after dark and avoid walking alone even in the daylight. If you're in a grocery store, you have every right to ask someone who works there to walk you to your car. Even if you didn't see anyone suspicious, the workers should be happy to make sure you make it to your car safely. If you're leaving work, and your car is parked in a place that is a bit far from the entrance, ask a co-worker to go with you. It's better to look silly for being paranoid than to end up on missing posters.

Protect Your Mind

What you watch, what you think about, and what you listen to all have incredible influence on your mental wellbeing. Music and other people's words influence your way of thinking. Social media is one of the biggest places people lose themselves in the sea of voices all shouting about who you should be, how you should look, or what you should believe in. Society's expectations are one of the top destroyers of uniqueness and individuality.

> *"Finally, brothers, whatever is true, whatever is noble, whatever is right, whatever is pure, whatever is lovely, whatever is admirable—if anything is excellent or praiseworthy—think about such things."*
> *Philippians 4:8*

Remaining positive is one of the most challenging things we face on a day-to-day basis. I like to complain. ... I mean, I don't LIKE to complain, but it comes so naturally. If I've got something to complain about, I find myself looking for someone to complain to.

I watched a show once which really drove this point home for me. It was a series about female teen athletes. I was interested in their progress as they worked toward their goals to become Olympians. These girls had bad attitudes. They were competing for each other's boyfriends and backbiting each other in order to gain what they saw as power and control. What I didn't realize was that the more I got into the show, the more my own personal attitude started to change. I began to be more testy and less forgiving of people around me. When I finally recognized the change in my attitude and behavior, I realized I needed to pull back on shows like this. Very quickly, I started becoming myself again.

One of the most powerful things to bring about a change in attitude has to do with the music you listen to or the shows and movies you watch. They can be categorized into three different groups. Twinkie music, rocks & dirt, and fruits and veggies.

A Twinkie here and there will not kill you and is a nice treat. But a steady diet of Twinkies will slowly give you health problems … some of which can be deadly. This is the same as just listening to pointless or lighthearted songs or watching too many movies or shows with shallow messages. A few here and there are fun and up-lifting. But a steady diet of those without balancing out your spiritual intake with good wholesome music and media will slowly drag you down. Your perspective of reality will be warped, and your expectations on family, friends, or yourself can become unrealistic. You can find yourself becoming short tempered when people don't respond to you or making decisions the way you think they should. This is because people are less predictable than they are in the movies. Movies and shows are scripted to be entertainment or set standards of how people should react to certain situations in order to bring the most amount of entertainment to their audience. Bottom line, you can't expect reality to look like what you see in the media. Not even "reality TV" is "realistic."

Everyone knows that eating rocks and dirt will kill you. But how much of our music and entertainment intake would fall under the "rocks and dirt" category? If we're honest, we definitely intake more than we should.

Most secular music has really poor messages, and most movies and shows promote shallow relationships, one-night stands, unfaithfulness in relationships, or hate and revenge. They're depressing, or oppressive. Take a look at the lyrics of your favorite songs. How many of them promote shallow relationships, breakups, hate, or vengeance? How many of them are degrading to men or women? How many are used to put yourself down… or to lift yourself up to the point that others don't matter? Or how many of them raise expectations that no man or woman can attain to?

Look at the movies and shows you watch… Really look at them. Do you really think you can learn how to have a long lasting and healthy marriage based on what you see in the media? Your average chick flick will tell the story of a woman who is stuck in a bad relationship and ends up leaving the man she's with for the "perfect man." They both live happily ever after. But look around you. How many relationships have you seen or been in that end like this? More often than not the new relationship which was supposed to be "happily ever after" just turns into the same old type of relationship and the cycle starts all over again. An endless, pointless, and depressing search for the perfect relationship among imperfect people.

So, how do we protect our minds? It's more than just moving away from rocks and dirt and twinkies. If you have a steady diet of fruits and veggies you will feel happy, healthy and energetic. It's the same with wholesome music and media. If you give your spirit a steady diet of godly music and shows or music with specifically positive messages, you'll feel happy, healthy, and energetic. When you're having a bad day, put on some godly music and your spirits will lift. When you're feeling bad about yourself, put on some music that speaks about who you were created to be and your self image will receive a boost. When you're depressed and feel that there is no good in the world, put on some music that tells about how great God is and your perspective will begin to change. Did you just experience a breakup? Put on something that tells about how much God loves you and cares for you. Your heart will begin to heal. Did someone close to you die? Put on something that sings of heaven, and your hope of reuniting with your loved one will spark a little.

Listening to things that feed the negativity you feel can help you feel justified with your feelings but will ultimately not make you actually feel better. Pour into yourself things that are positive and tell the truth of who you are, who God is, and how much He loves you and the people around you. In this way, you will protect your mind from negativity which will drag your mind deep into a dark place that will consume you and destroy your life.

Protect Your Spirit

Finally, be strong in the Lord and in His mighty power. Put on the full armor of God, so that you can take your stand against the devil's schemes. For our struggle is not against flesh and blood, but against the rulers, against the authorities, against the powers of this dark world and against the spiritual forces of evil in the heavenly realms. Therefore, put on the full armor of God, So that when the day of evil comes, you may be able to stand your ground. And after you have done everything, to stand. Stand firm then, with the belt of truth buckled around your waist, With the breastplate of righteousness in place,

And with your feet fitted with the readiness
that comes from the gospel of peace.
In addition to all this, take up the shield of faith,
With which you can extinguish all the
flaming arrows of the evil one.
Take the helmet of salvation and the sword of the spirit,
Which is the Word of God.

*"And pray in the Spirit on all occasions with all kinds
of prayers and requests. With this in mind, be alert and
always keep on praying for all the Lord's people."
Ephesians 6:8-10*

In this passage, the Bible talks about protection for your spirit as being like armor. It explains that the troubles we go through are due to a spiritual battle against Satan. We protect ourselves by covering ourselves with pieces of "spiritual armor." Truth, the Gospel, faith, salvation, the word of God (The Bible), and prayer. We protect our spirit by understanding that there is a God who holds all truth and the answers for every battle we face here on earth.

Cultivate your relationship with God. This is where you will find exactly how unique and incredible you were created to be. He will give you purpose in a world that screams that you are only as good as your looks or accomplishments. He will give you value in a world that places your value on what you own or how much money you have. He will put meaning in your life in a world where everything is meaningless.

The truth of God says that you are priceless, and irreplaceable. If you give God your whole heart, you will find yourself as you lose interest in what the world has to offer. He will give you goals and dreams that are so far beyond your imagination that it will blow your mind as you watch them come true.

How do you cultivate your relationship with God? This is something that many people miss altogether. They say, "I believe in God," I pray all the time," "I go to church," or "I read the Bible," but truly miss the point of an actual relationship with God.

> *"Faith is the substance of things hoped for and the evidence of things not seen."*
> *Hebrews 11:1*

Many people confuse faith with hope. We hope that the weather will be good for our picnic. We hope that we will be able to go to the concert. We hope that we will find a guy that will love us forever. But hope is only part of the definition of faith. Faith is more of a "knowing" combined with an action.

When you prepare to sit on a chair, you have faith that the chair will hold you. How do you know that you have faith? First, you are confident in the chair's strength and balanced foundation to be able to hold you. Second, you act out your confidence by actually sitting on the chair. You don't feel it first or push it around to make sure that it's solid. You just sit.

So let's break it down according to what the Hebrews 11:1 tells faith in God is:

"The substance of things hoped for." – Peace in knowing that no matter what happens in this life, God is still good and still has plans to prosper me and not to harm me, plans to give me hope and a future.

"The evidence of things not seen." – Living for Christ even when the world thinks I'm crazy. Being a disciple of Jesus because I believe that He is God and that He sacrificed His life to save mine on the cross.

The Substance of faith is God's work in me. The Evidence of faith is His work through me. It takes both to make faith. You can't have one without the other or faith would be incomplete.

So, how do you apply this truth to your life? Don't just pray to God. Listen to what He has to say to you. Don't just read your Bible. Study it to learn what God has to teach you in it's pages. Don't just go to church. Get involved in one way or another. Join extra Bible studies or ministry opportunities as they come up. Fellowship with other believers so that you can learn from them, and they can learn from you. Don't do good things or be kind and caring because you want people to know that you're a good person. Do them because it's the right thing to do. Do them even when no one knows you're doing them just because you know God will be pleased. Don't harbor any kind of hate or unforgiveness toward anyone. Let those things go and let love fill your heart for everyone around you… even those who hurt you or mean you ill will. Fill your mind with godly things and the good things God has offered to you, and your spirit will be protected.

Protect Your Body

Society tells you all about what you should wear, how you should look, what your body type should be… It's all superficial. But the truth is how you treat your body can tell a lot about how you value yourself as a person. Wearing certain styles "because they're in" starts to strip away at your uniqueness. Wearing styles that you are comfortable in and make you feel like yourself (weather they are "in style" or not), makes a statement that you're happy with who you are.
I know some of you may not want to hear it but wearing revealing clothing is not about being unique or comfortable

with your body. If you're honest with yourself, you know that if you wear revealing clothing it's because you want to be looked at. Getting mad at someone for looking at you is hypocritical. You put it on knowing full well that you were going to turn heads. It's why you wore it in the first place.

Let me be abundantly clear. I'm not saying you're asking to be sexually harassed in any way. Every man should have the respect and decency to keep his hands and rude comments to himself. If he does not, he is in the wrong and you should get mad. Very mad. But listen ladies. By nature, guys are much more visually driven than we are. You know that even as a girl you can't keep from noticing another girl who is wearing revealing clothing. How on earth can you expect a guy to keep his eyes on your face if your bikini is barely holding your boobs in or your shorts come within a few centimeters of your butt cheeks? Wearing revealing clothing is rude and disrespectful to yourself, your own value, and to every guy you come across.

It's like going up to your best friend, who you know is trying to eat healthy, and putting her favorite ice cream within inches of her face. She knows she can't have it…you know she can't have it…but you do it anyway, and then eat the ice cream in front of her.

If you truly respect your guy friends, you will find ways to dress that make you feel confident and even sexy without showing off your body in such a way that guys can't see you for your wonderful personality. Showing off your boobs is cheating others out of knowing you as a person. Showing off your butt with your short shorts is cheating you out of knowing if a guy likes you for who you are or just for what he thinks you have to offer. Even showing off your sexy tummy can draw a guy's attention away from who you are.

Did you know that the sexier you dress, the shallower your

relationships will be? The more you reveal about your body, the more guys you will attract that care less about your hopes and dreams and more about sex. Did you know that you really can attract guys that care about who you are, how intelligent you are, what your plans for your future are, and what you believe in? Would you like to attract a guy like that?

They say in the work force to "dress for the position you want." Do you want the position of a confident and powerful woman who has a strong and committed relationship with a solid man who won't go looking for the next sexy piece of meat? Dress your body type to be stylish and sexy without being revealing. You'll attract a much better caliber of men.

Protect Your Health

Now let's talk about health. This has nothing to do with your size or shape! If everyone had the exact same figure and/or BMI, we would live in a very boring world. God made people of different shapes and sizes in order to keep things interesting! In some parts of the world, thin and small is considered beautiful. In other parts of the world, it's a sign of health to have more meat on your bones. In some cultures, it's normal to be tall. In some it's normal to be short. And guess what? God gave each person their own personality that will be attracted to different kinds of beauty. Some guys like "thicker" women. Some guys like taller women. Some like bigger butts, some like bigger boobs. Some like smaller breasts. Some like longer legs. The point is, God made your body perfectly just the way it is, and the right guy will be attracted to you exactly how God made you. So, when I talk about health, I'm not talking about the number on the scale or the size of your jeans.

Eat right and exercise. You've heard it a thousand times. I know you have because every health and fitness commercial out there pushes these points. They're right. If you're eating healthy, exercising regularly, and getting enough rest, you're giving your body the best chance at warding off sickness, viruses, and diseases. It's not a guarantee that you won't get sick, but it lowers your risks. It's also not a guarantee that you will ever fit into a size 0 pants, so unless your body type actually fits into something that small, just let it go. Focus on eating foods that are as close to the earth as possible, like fruits, vegetables, and real meats. Processed lunch meats and meats with fillers and tons of breading are not as healthy as you think. I'm not saying that you should boycott pizza or anything, just be more aware of what you eat, how much you eat it, and where it came from. The majority of your food intake should be as healthy as possible, and indulgences like ice cream and soda should be more like an every-once-in-a-while treat. If you take care of your body properly, you will end up with the body frame God has designed for you. Be proud of it. Own it. Dress for your body type and be confident. True confidence (not flashiness) is sexy and can help attract the right kind of guys.

Protect Your Reputation

Who you hang out with, what you say, what you do and, how you treat people, will tell a lot about who you are. If you gossip, you will attract people who will gossip about you. If you cheat on your boyfriend, you will attract the kind of guys who are likely to cheat on you. If you are rude, you will attract people who will be rude to you. But, if you are kind, you will attract kind people. If you are loving, you will attract loving people. If you are loyal, you will attract loyal people. Also remember that even when you don't know it, you are being an example to younger people of how they should be as they grow up.

Protect Your Online Presence

Do not give your passwords out to anyone except for a trusted parent or guardian. In the wrong hands, passwords can give people power over your life and your reputation.

Do not post sexy pictures of yourself or send them to anyone, not even your best friend or your boyfriend. You should literally not trust anyone with this kind of power over you, and you should never trust yourself with that kind of power over anyone else. Anything can happen. You and your boyfriend could break up, and he could send that picture or post it for thousands of people to see. You and your friend could get into a huge fight, and she could do some incredible damage to you and your reputation. It doesn't matter if you feel that these people would never do that. Remember, they are human and are capable of doing anything. And even if they really wouldn't, they might know people who would, and that person can get ahold of your picture and ruin your reputation.

Trust me, this is not the kind of thing you want out there. Once something is out there on the internet, even paid professionals have no control over how far it can go. Even if pictures are taken down, people can take screen shots and keep them circulating. This can affect your safety and your future for years to come. There are people who have been denied scholarships and jobs over sexy or questionable pictures out on the internet. This includes pictures of people doing stupid things at parties. The internet can take one small stupid mistake and ruin your life with it.

Do not talk with anyone online who you do not personally know and trust. I'm talking about people who you have met in person and who your parents or trusted adults know and trust. I know girls personally who have been sexually exploited online and over the phone. It was a nightmare for them and will be a nightmare for you. It starts small. "Send me a pic of you."

Then "Send me a pic of your legs." Then, "Send me a pic of your butt in your favorite shorts." Then, your bathing suit, then your underwear...He will push it as far as he can. With each picture you send, he gains mor and more power to blackmail you if you don't give him the next thing he wants.

Make sure your parents or a trusted adult knows about every person you have contact with online. If you ever go missing, this will be one of the first places they will start to try to find you and rescue you. And if you and your trusted adult are careful enough, no one will ever be able to target you online.

Protect Your Family

Honor your father and mother is one of God's commandments. It comes with a promise that God will bless you. Does this mean that you should do everything your parents tell you to do even if it's wrong or goes against what the Bible says to be right? Absolutely not. If your parents step outside of God's will, you are still accountable to God Himself and should follow God's leading. It does mean that you should speak respectfully to them and about them. You should do whatever you can to honor the good lessons they have taught you in life and pass on those lessons to your children. It means that you should listen to them respectfully and take whatever wisdom they have to offer. Don't talk bad about your family unless there is a real problem and you need help. And then, only talk to a trusted and wise person who has the power to do something about your situation.

You should also protect your siblings. If you see them doing something that will harm them, speak up! If you see someone in their life that is toxic, let them know what you see. If someone bullies them, step in. Love and respect your siblings and they will love and respect you. Be a team, and they will always have your back.

Protect Your Friendships

Treat your friends with love, kindness, and loyalty and you will develop some really amazing friendships that can last a lifetime. Build your friends up, and never tear them down even in joking. You never know when you might hit a trigger for them and deeply hurt them. Talk about the things you like about them, and never put down any physical feature.

Protect Your Relationship

Be loyal to your boyfriend. Protect his mind by being careful about what your wear around him. If you would not wear something in front of your dad or big brother, don't wear it in front of your boyfriend. This can awaken feelings in him that can ruin your time together because he will be too conscious about what's going on inside his mind to enjoy the time he has with you. He can be too distracted by your body to have the kind of meaningful conversations which can give you the opportunity to get to know who he is.

"I charge you, O daughters of Jerusalem...Do not stir up or awaken love before it's time."
Song of Solomon 8:4

What does this mean? It means do not flirt with a man that is not your husband to the point of seduction. Do not reveal too much of your sexuality to him and stir up sexual feelings in him or yourself. Take the important time to get to know each other, and if you decide to get married, allow those sexual desires to be "awakened" on your wedding night. Believe me, the wait is worth it.

Be watchful of how much attention you give other guys. While it is perfectly fine and healthy to have friendships with other guys, it is not respectful to them or your boyfriend to give them a lot of attention, flirt with them, or confide in them things you wouldn't say to your boyfriend.

Communicate with your boyfriend. This is incredibly important. Communicate about how the relationship is going. Be truthful about who you are and how you're feeling. If you hide who you really are, how will he know if you are the one for him? If he hides who he is, how will you know if this is someone you can spend the rest of your life with? But, remember this. If it turns out that you two are really not good together as a couple, you need to be willing to let him go. He also needs to be willing to let you go.

Remember this, ladies ... boyfriends do not get husband rights. This is one of the most important things to remember but also one of the most misunderstood concepts in society. It's something that has cheapened sex, relationships, and marriages to the point that they don't hold hardly any value. Here is the truth. ... A boyfriend has no right to your personal property, your home, your bed, or your body. If he wants it, he'd better put a ring on it and be faithful and committed to you and your relationship until death do you part.

Guard your heart, beautiful one. It's precious and easily broken. Don't let just anyone hold it. Others don't understand how precious it is to you. And guard the heart of your future husband. His heart is just as precious. Remember, things that you do today can hurt him in the future.

Love Always Trusts

Chapter 14

Verb: 'To believe in the reliability, truth, ability, or strength of something or someone.'

My Story

It's such a good thing I didn't try to write my love story by myself! I love my story. God planned out everything perfectly. But that doesn't mean that my lessons in trust were done. As I said before, I knew that God was preparing me to be someone's second chance. When Frankie came into my life, I had to learn a whole new level of trust. Several in fact. I had to grow deeper in my faith in God and at the same time build trust with Frankie.

Frankie had gone down some very dark roads before he finally met God and surrendered his life to Him. While he was at his lowest and asking God to fix all of his problems, he finally looked up and saw a God who had sacrificed everything for him. He realized that he was making empty promises to a loving and forgiving God. He was asking God to be ok with his sin and let him "off the hook" so that he could go back and keep right on living in all of the sin that Jesus had died to free him from. It broke him.

From that day forward, Frankie determined that he was going to live his life for God. He started studying his Bible and learning from other godly men. He worked in ministries and even led some classes. He knew that if he studied God's Word, I mean really studied it, the Holy Spirit would reveal Truth to him, and that's all he wanted.

Frankie started to desire a Godly wife. But who would take someone with this brokenness? He brought his concerns to God. He told God that he would be happy with a wife who was just as broken as he was with just as dark a past. He would be satisfied to live with her in a shack, as long as she was the one God had for him. But we serve a God of second chances. A God who restores so much more than we lose due to our own shortcomings. All we have to do is trust Him.

God is Trustworthy

Trust is so essential to life. We need to be able to trust in the people around us in order to be comfortable and confident in our surroundings. Take a look at the trust of a child... ready to jump off of something high into the arms of their mother or father. They don't worry if they will be caught or not. They trust completely that the arms of the one who loves them wouldn't dare let them fall. Most children are not worried about where they are going to get clothes. Many take for granted that food will always be readily available. God asks us to trust Him like that. Faith like a child.

> *"He called a little child to Him, and placed the child among them. And He said: "Truly I tell you, unless you change and become like little children, you will never enter the kingdom of heaven."*
> *Matthew 18:2-4*

This is the kind of childlike trust God asks us to have for Him. The thing is, He is trustworthy and won't let you down. He created you with needs and loves you more than anything. He will follow through with His promises. He will catch you if you fall. He will provide for your needs.

> *"Therefore I tell you, do not worry about your life, what you will eat or drink; or about your body, what you will wear. Is not life more than food, and the body more than clothes? Look at the birds of the air; they do not sow or reap or store away in barns, and yet your Heavenly Father feeds them. Are you not much more valuable than they?"*
> *Matthew 6:25-26*

> *"And why do you worry about clothes? See how the flowers of the field grow. They do not labor or spin. Yet I tell you that not even Solomon in all his splendor was dressed like one of these."*
> *Matthew 6:28-29*

Does this mean that He's going to give you high end clothing, gourmet food and you'll be rich? Nope. That's not what it's saying. Not that having those things is wrong, but His promise is to provide for you what you need. If you trust in Him, He will meet your daily needs, your emotional needs, and your spiritual needs.

Notice the "if" part. It takes faith. Trust that God loves you and wants the best for you. Work on your relationship with Him so that you get to know Him better and can understand when He is asking you to step out and do something. Be obedient to His Word. And whatever you need that you cannot provide for yourself, He will step in and make a way to provide for you.

"And my God will supply all your need according to His riches in glory by Jesus Christ."
Philippians 4:19

"But seek first His kingdom and His righteousness and all these things will be given to you as well."
Matthew 6:33

Sometimes trusting in God's plan for your life doesn't make sense. Sometimes He asks us to do something that seems counter intuitive. He's done it many times throughout history. He asked Abraham to be willing to sacrifice his only son as a burnt offering. This was a test of his faith and obedience, but it was more than that. God was giving a hint of what He was going to do in order to save us from our sins. He was showing that no mere human was good enough to be a sacrifice for our sins. Just as God provided a ram for Abraham to sacrifice in place of his only son, God's only Son, Jesus would be sacrificed in our place for the forgiveness of our sin and restore our pure relationship with God forever.

God asked Moses to speak to a rock in order to provide water to thousands of people. He asked Joshua to march around a city and scream at the walls in order for the walls to come down so they could take the city. Jesus spit in dirt to make mud and put it on someone's eyes to heal him so he could see again! Strange things. But because of their faith and because they trusted that He is faithful to do what He says He will do even when it doesn't make sense, God accomplished many amazing things.

"Trust in the Lord with all your heart, and lean not on your own understanding. In all your ways

acknowledge Him, and he shall direct your paths."
Proverbs 3:5-6

Trust in Friendship Relationships

Nearly all definitions of trust imply expectations of some kind. We expect that the person we trust will not take advantage of us. We expect that they will react in one way or another to any given situation. But expectations can be dangerous. Putting expectations on people usually ends up in disappointment. People are different, think differently, react differently, and have free will. Not everyone will react the way you want or expect them to. In fact, they usually won't. This can make trust difficult to build between people. Though not impossible.

So, should you ignore someone's past and just trust that they are who they say they are? Not necessarily. The point of my story is that I trusted God more than man and followed His lead. Trust in relationships needs to be accompanied by wisdom. God is perfect. People are not. Blind trust in people is simply not wise and will end in frustrations and broken relationships. The truth is that people will let you down in one way or another. This is guaranteed. God never will. If you put your relationships in God's hands, He will guide you. He will either show you when you need to step away from a relationship or He will show you how to strengthen a relationship to make it better.

Have you ever met someone who is really trustworthy? This person is known for doing what they say they're going to do. They're always where they say they're going to be. They are true to who they are and act the same no matter who they are around. These trustworthy people tend to be very successful in life. They tend to get promoted at their jobs and are trusted with important things. These are people you should be looking up to and striving to be like.

If you were to ask the employees of some of the most successful billionaires in the world, many would tell you that their employer's success was built on the integrity of the business owner. What is integrity? It's being honest and having strong moral standards and principles. These are qualities you need to cultivate and develop in your own life in order to be successful and trustworthy.

In addition, you need to surround yourself with trustworthy people. If you hang around people who are dishonest, flaky, or unreliable, others won't trust you just because of association. Even if you consider yourself trustworthy and true to yourself no matter who you are around, others won't see it that way. This can hurt your chances at being trusted with important things. If you're living at home, your parents may find it difficult to let you use the car or go somewhere on your own. Even if you promise to be responsible and careful, if they can't trust the people you are hanging out with, it can be difficult for them to allow you those privileges. It can hinder you from getting a job or being promoted.

The more you hang around untrustworthy people, the more you will start to become like them. If they don't care about curfew, it will be easy for you to start to miss your own curfew. If they lie to their parents, they might pressure you to lie to yours. The more they push, the more you will question your strong morals and start to lower your standards. You'll wonder if it really is that bad to just tell your parents you'll be one place and go somewhere else. You won't be "lying" because you'll be there for a short time. They'll never know anyway. But trust me, you don't want to start down this path. Once you do, lying gets easier and easier and the boundaries of what you know is right will be pushed further and further until you no longer have the security of those boundaries and you've pushed something too far. Someone could get hurt, or you lose someone's trust forever.

So, do what you say you're going to do. Be who you say you are. Be honest and trustworthy. Make friends who also hold these standards for themselves. As you strengthen relationships with people who are more like who you want to be, you can slowly pull away from the old "life" and old "friends." You'll like who you become, and others will too.

Trust in Romantic Relationships

When it comes to trust in a romantic relationship there are many things to consider. How well do you know this person? How do you know if he is trustworthy or not? Watch him closely. Does he say one thing then do another? Does he tell his parents that he's going to do chores then blow them off for something more interesting? If given the opportunity, would he cheat? Is he comfortable with telling "white lies" or "little lies" to get out of one thing or another or to soften the truth to make it more acceptable? Does he consistently make excuses for himself in order to not take responsibility for his own actions?

Some people who are not trustworthy are particularly distrustful of others. They have a hard time believing that people will not let them down because they are not committed to their own word and they believe that others are the same way. These are red flags and should not be ignored.

This is not to say that a trustworthy person can't have trust issues as well. Someone who has been let down or abused in the past will very often have a problem believing that there are people out there that can be trusted. This is a matter of being healed from past hurts and finding friends with integrity who will help gain the trust of the victim.

The bottom line is that you need to be a trustworthy person and surround yourself with trustworthy people. Trust God with the rest.

Love Always Hopes

Chapter 15

Noun: 'a feeling of expectation and desire for a certain thing to happen.'

My Story

In January 2009, our family had a breakthrough. My dad was still not ok with us getting married yet, but I had done everything I could possibly do to honor him as my father, and he wasn't budging. God gave me the assurance I needed to move forward with planning our wedding. We planned it for May 23rd, 2009. I spent the next 4 months driving myself absolutely crazy planning our wedding. Thankfully, during this time, Frankie and I didn't have a ton of time to get into too much trouble physically.

The dress I had made was almost perfect. The train was a little shorter than I had wanted, and there were embellishments that still needed to be finished. But, I was a seamstress! Even though I didn't have the confidence to make my dress from scratch, I had the skills needed to do whatever alterations I desired. So, I altered the train, and added the vines and beading I had seen in my dream when I was 12. It was my wedding dress, and it was perfect!

I worked with my decorator to plan the backdrop at the alter, and she took it so much further and made it so much more beautiful than I had imagined! I spent a few days working with friends to decorate and hang twinkle lights up in the reception area. When the power went out 4 days before the wedding (which required

2 days for the power company to fix), a couple of the men in the church brought generators and set them up so that we could make sure everything was perfect for the big day. I don't think I ever thanked them properly for jumping in to save the day.

Our wedding day finally came! It was a magical day with family and friends. I got up early to have my hair professionally done and headed to the church where my wonderful wedding party was waiting. My sister-in-law did my makeup, my friends helped me with the lacing on the back of my dress and getting my shoes on. When an accident happened that could have ruined my dress, my beautiful maid of honor helped keep me calm while my friends took care of the spill so that it would not show up on my dress...just in time for the ceremony to start.

In all its imperfections, it was a perfect ceremony. There were twinkle lights, tulle, and purple roses everywhere. Frankie and I had written our wedding vows into a song which we sang to each other as my mom and her friend accompanied us on guitar and piano. My husband's goofy groomsmen pretended to lose the wedding rings in a perfectly comical act. Our wonderful pastors officiated the ceremony, and with the official signing of the marriage certificate, we shared our very first real kiss. It was amazing.

Even though he did not walk me down the aisle, my Dad did come to the wedding and witnessed one of the most important days of my life. He also danced with me during the father/daughter dance, and even gave us money toward our honeymoon with a statement to my mom that now that we were married, it was their job to make sure we had a good marriage. For me, it was hope realized.

God Brings Hope

Hope is often misunderstood to be more like a wish. But hope is much deeper than that. A wish is putting a desire out there and not being sure that it will ever come true. Hope is an assurance that something is going to happen and being excited and anticipating for it to come. It's more of an "I can't wait!"

God talks about hope throughout the Bible! In the Old Testament, Abraham was asked to leave everything behind to travel with his wife to some far off country that God would reveal to him later. The promised land of Canaan which would eventually become the land of Israel. Women like Sarah and Hannah were given the hope of being able to bear children even though they were unable to for many years. Esther was able to change a law and give her people hope that they would not be annihilated but would be allowed to defend themselves. Ruth was given the hope of a new life with her mother-in-law, and because of her faithfulness, was given the honor of being the great grandmother of King David from whom eventually came the savior of the World. Hope was given to the children of Israel that a redeemer would come and save them. In the New Testament, that hope was finally fulfilled with Jesus' coming. Through Jesus we have the best hope of all. Hope of living forever in Heaven!

Hope For Your Future

So, when it comes to hope in relationships, I want you to start hoping for your future. I want you to hope for a good man. I want you to hope for a good marriage. I want you to dream about what your life might look like together.

It's time to dream like the princess you are!

Close your eyes and think of your future mate. What does he look like physically? Does he have dark hair? Light hair? No hair? Is he tall or short? Is he muscular or thinner? Does he have brown, blue, or green eyes?

How about intellectually or in regards to work ethic? Would you like him to have or be working towards a college degree? Would you rather he be interested in a trade? Does it matter to you? Would you rather be the breadwinner and he stay home with the kids, or would you like his career to support you being a full-time mom?

Describe his personality. Do you like the strong silent type? How about the goofy jokester type? Are you looking for someone more introverted or extroverted?

What hobbies might he have? Is he into sports? Does he like to fish, mountain bike, hike, or ride motorcycles? Is he a musician? Does he love to read or play chess? Are you a gamer looking for another gamer?

What does your dream home look like? Are you more of an apartment in the city girl or an acres of land country girl? Does the white picket fence clean cut lawns suburbs sound like the best of both worlds to you?

How will he act towards his family? Your family? Your friends? Your future children? Does he even want children, and if so, how many? How will he act towards you emotionally and romantically? Will he support as you pursue your passions and/or career? How will he deal with conflicts or major life decisions?

These are all fun things to think about! But, many of those qualities or traits may not end up describing your future husband. And that's ok! Life is full of surprises, and God loves to give us things that are even better than we thought we wanted. And in other ways, He likes to challenge us to compromise and grow to appreciate that He has the best for us. These things help us to mature as people. For instance, I thought I would find my husband while living on my own in Colorado. Turns out, I found him while living back at home in California with my parents. And I couldn't be happier now.

Let's dig a little deeper. When considering spending the rest of your life with someone, it's always wise to consider qualities you feel they absolutely must have and traits they must not have to be able to live with you harmoniously. Some of the things you just imagined about your future husband are extremely important and would be deal breakers if they don't line up with your desires. Some of them are "would be nice to have" types of things.

So, let's break it down. What are the most important things you're looking for in a husband? This is your "must have" category These are the deal breakers. If these qualities or traits aren't met, the relationship is dead in the water. As I said before, my top three priorities were that he love God first, then me and our future children second, and love ministry third. I would not marry a man who wasn't like this. If you absolutely must have a man that is a hard worker, put it in your "must have" category. If he must be kind and forgiving, be a good money manager, be trustworthy, humble, or a good communicator, list those out. Include your morals and spiritual beliefs. If his morals and spiritual beliefs do not line up with yours, you are in for a really bumpy ride.

Next is your "must not have" category. It's important to really think this through and only list things that you absolutely won't compromise on. For example, if you hate cigarette smoke, don't think he'll quit for you. If you do not want to live with someone with an anger problem, don't think that if he's a hot head now he will mellow out over time. If you've been traumatized because of growing up around abuse or drugs, do not think that you can save him from that lifestyle. Put all these in your "must not have" category.

Now that you've built the perfect guy, let's dream about life. How do you imagine meeting him? Have you been friends since you were little and begin to realize that you've had feelings for each other all your life? Did you meet at a football game with your friends? Was he the quiet guy in class that needed help with a science project? Was he the outspoken guy in youth group who loves to talk about God to anyone who will listen? Is it love at first sight, or do you grow to love each other over time?

What's your idea of the perfect date? Would you like to dress up and go to a fancy restaurant? Would you prefer pizza at the favorite local pizza place? How about ice skating or going to a hockey game? How about miniature golf or bumper cars?

While you're getting to know each other, how do you imagine spending time together? Come up with things that are fun and really allow you to talk and get to know each other. Spend lots of time with friends or at least around other people to discourage getting too close physically. If you like gaming together, just make sure you're not alone in the house and that the door is open if the game room is separated from the rest of the house, Do you like the idea of reading together? Do you love playing board games, hanging out with friends at the pool or hanging out at the mall?

What is your idea of a perfect proposal? Do you like grand gestures like flash mobs or carriage rides? Do you prefer intimate proposals like fancy dinners or walks on the beach? Would you like your family to be there? Do you imagine him getting on one knee? Would you like to break with tradition and be the one to pop the question yourself? Make sure your friends and family know what kind of proposal you like! Your future husband will likely ask them for some advice, so you want them to have a heads up!

Dream of your perfect wedding. What does your dream wedding dress look like? Which styles of wedding rings do you like? What colors do you want at your wedding? Who do you imagine standing with you in your bridal party? What kind of flowers do you like? Do you want twinkle lights? Does a day wedding or an evening wedding sound more fun? Would you rather do something crazy like getting married while scuba diving?

What will life together with your future husband look like? Will you stay close to your hometown or go travel the world? Will you both go into high end careers? Would you like to become homesteaders? Will you have children? If so, how many and how far apart would you like them to be? Will you choose public school, private school, or homeschool for them? What kinds of memories would you like to make as a family?

Dream about your future! Hope for all that God has for you and watch as He writes an amazing and exciting life with ups and downs great accomplishments and successes. Watch as he takes your failures and the things that life throws at you and uses them to help you to grow and mature as individuals and as a couple.

Now, let's come down from the clouds. I want to talk about the here and now. I believe with all my heart that it's important to dream about the future and keep a watchful eye out for everything that God is working on for you. But equally as important is what you're doing now and what God has for you now. I do not want you to get so caught up in looking for your perfect match that you miss everything God has for you in your singleness. I really want you to enjoy your independent life! Marriage isn't the ultimate goal in life. Having kids isn't your whole purpose for living! Once you're married, your attention and your desires will shift from what's best for you to what's best for both of you and eventually what's best for your kids as well.

Now is an incredibly important time for you to get to know who you are and find out what you like and dislike. Develop into a powerful woman of God who knows her worth and doesn't need a man to validate her. Order Chinese for yourself and don't worry about having to ask someone if they would prefer pizza. Watch that chick flick that your future husband wouldn't want to watch with you. Plan that trip, go to that college, build that career, make those friends, get that job and rent that apartment all on your own. Save the money and buy that car. Find the strong and independent woman in you that doesn't need a man to fulfill you or support you. Then, when you really are ready, God will bring about the right guy. Either you'll find him among your friends, or he'll show up out of nowhere. You may even decide it's time to date and you'll find him on a dating app. He may be the car salesman after you've saved up to buy that car. He might be the bank employee that help you set up a savings account. He might be the drummer from your church band.

I don't know what God's story for you is, but I know that if you find your self worth in God and your independence away from men before you jump into dating, you'll be stronger and more stable and able to set up a solid foundation for a marriage built on trust and respect. You won't need your husband you'll want him. You won't be dependent on him for survival, you'll trust him to build a life with you. You never know where he might turn up, but you do not need to sit back and wait for him to come! Keep busy! Hang around the kind of people with similar and healthy goals and interests. Spend time with people who share your your morals and your spiritual beliefs. Somewhere in there, you'll start to notice that someone is running the same race you are...and he's kind of cute too.

Even though I decided that I didn't want to date until I found the man I would marry, I do not want you to think that you must walk that same road. That was a personal thing between me and God, and He fulfilled my request. It's ok to date! It's ok to get to know someone and then find out that you have different wants and desires. Not every relationship before marriage has to end up being a bad thing. Some guys you might date will be really great but just not the right one for you. Some breakups will be harder than others. Some will leave your heartbroken and some will be mutual partings that leave you a bit sad, but glad you didn't get too invested. But what's important for you to do is to change the mindset that dating is just meaningless fun. If you date at all, your intention should be to find out if you are compatible with him enough to begin to look at building a life together.

Love Always Perseveres

Chapter 16

Verb: 'To continue in a course of action even in the face of difficulty or with little or no prospect of success.'

My Story

We took off to our honeymoon in a convertible someone had rented for us. I was happy but so nervous the whole way. I was going to be giving my virginity to the man of my dreams (literally). As we got closer to the coast, my nervousness began to be overshadowed by something else… the temperature was dropping. It was May, but the temperature at the coast was in the 40s! My wonderful new husband searched for a thrift store where we could buy some cheap warm clothes, because we had packed for warm weather. Afterwards, we found our hotel, went for a wonderful fancy dinner at a restaurant that overlooked the ocean during the sunset, and headed back to the hotel for "the big night." I was so nervous!

I spent a bunch of time in the bathroom taking bobby pins out of my hair, taking a shower, and putting on the special nightgown I had brought for that night. I was still so very nervous, but also excited. When I came out of the bathroom to my new husband, he looked on me with such love. He really was the man of my dreams. He was the perfect gentleman, kind, and caring with me as we shared the wonderful gift that God had given us. Unity of body and spirit.

Then, I slept in bed with a man for the first time in my life. My gift from God, my husband … I woke up in the middle of the night freezing … he had thrown all of the blankets off the other side of the bed, and I was too nervous as a new bride to do anything about it. He felt so bad in the morning, but I will just tuck it away as a hilarious end to my first night as a wife.

I realized that one of the reasons God planned for us to save sex for marriage was because when that physical connection was made, a spiritual connection was also formed. If we had made that connection and then had decided (for any reason) not to go through with our marriage, the pain would have been excruciating. If we had called it off before that connection was made, a loss would have been felt, but if we would have given in to our sexual desires and become unified in body and spirit, it would have torn into our spirits and left scars.

I will never regret each difficult parting from my fiancée because the sexual tension was rising and if we were to remain pure until our wedding day, we had to get away from each other… immediately. But God honored our perseverance, and I will never regret presenting my new husband with my pure body the night after we exchanged vows before God. We were in this for the long haul… a life of unity before God…till death do us part.

God Will Pursue You Until the End

If you have stuck with me this far, I'm sure you understand that every piece of advice I have for relationships points back to your relationship with God. There is no way of finding true love within yourself or your relationships with anyone else if you do not understand God's love for you.

> "Behold, I stand at the door and knock. If anyone hears My voice and opens the door, I will come in to him and dine with him, and he with Me."

Revelation 3:20

I hope that you have opened your heart to Him. I hope you have found everything you have ever needed in His grace and mercy. I hope that your love story begins and ends with Jesus… the only one to love you so much that He left His throne in Heaven to come down to earth, be betrayed, beaten, ridiculed, and murdered to free you from all of the things that hold you down and hold you back from True Love. In exchange for our brokenness, He offers a peace unexplainable, joy inexpressible, strength insurmountable, and glory undeserved. I truly hope you choose Him.

I'm so glad God has stuck with me even in my stupidest moments in life. When I mess up and make a fool of myself, I get to where I don't want to talk to people anymore. What's the point? I'm just going to open my big mouth and say something dumb again. Either I'm going to hurt someone's feelings or give some bad advice. But God holds me close and tells me everything will be ok. He helps me to restore relationships wherever possible. He cleans the mud off of my face and teaches me how to handle the situation better next time. He is patient with me and lets me take tests over and over again until I pass. When I'm weak He is strong.

"And He said to me, "My grace is sufficient for you, for my strength is made perfect in weakness."
2 Corinthians 12:9

All I have to do is keep my focus on Him and He gives me the strength for everything He sets before me. The beauty of Godly perseverance is that it's not something I have to conjure up on my own. He is the one that gives me the strength I need to endure.

Persevering in Purity

There were so many times I wondered if finding a husband would ever happen for me. I looked for him everywhere. I looked among my friends and tried to decide if I liked any of them. I wondered from time to time if my standards really were too high. In fact, I have friends who later confessed that they thought that my standards were so high they believed that I would never get married! But, God had given me a promise when I was a teen. He had promised me that I would be someone's second chance. He put the desire in my heart for a godly man and a godly marriage. I dreamed of it. I hoped for it. I stood on the promise that God had the best plan for me. I persevered, and I finally achieved!

Was it easy? No. I felt like an outcast. I felt like a 3rd wheel. I felt unpopular. I felt alone and unwanted...even ugly and undesirable at times. The only way I was able to persevere was to push aside those thoughts and hold on to my stubborn determination to not lower my standards for anyone or anything. Even the thought of lowering my standards brought back memories of my mom and the many broken teenage hearts she had worked to help heal over the years. I was afraid that if I lowered my standards, I would end up with a broken heart myself. You see, fear is not always a bad thing! It kept my guard up and my heart protected. But it only worked because I had put my trust so completely in to my Creator's will for my life that I knew I would be ready to let those guards down when the time was right.

When I finally did open my heart to my future husband, my perseverance was tested once again as we got closer and closer. It wasn't easy to push him away when we were getting too close.

It was heart wrenching whenever we fought and it looked like each time would be the end of the relationship that we both had poured so much into. But, we both kept our eyes on Jesus, and He kept bringing us back together. He helped us work through our differences and weaknesses and gave us the strength to endure. We persevered and we made it. You can too!

The decisions you make now affect your future. So, make decisions you can be proud of. Make decisions that your future husband can be proud of! Until you are ready for marriage, don't just sit around waiting for Mr. Right to come along. Get a job. Work on a hobby. Go to school for something that you're passionate about. Don't go looking for romance. Look for true and solid friendships…the kind of friends who will have your back if you are in a relationship or not. The kind of friends that even if you move away from them, they will still love you and call you and want to get together when they're in town. These friendships are priceless and timeless.

Involve yourself in a church family. Go to the Bible Studies and learn from other believers. Help out in soup kitchens, food drives, clothing giveaways, and church functions. These things will get you around kind and generous people and will help you to learn more about yourself!

Persevering in Relationships

Finding your Prince Charming is only the beginning! Now it's time to spend the rest of your life getting to know each other. You will learn a lot about each other while you are dating, but you will learn far more about each other after you get married. And you will keep learning more about each other until you die. This is why it's so important to take it slow at the beginning and invest the time in learning as much about each other as you can before you get married.

After you get married, as you build your life together, you will find that you are both changing and adapting to each others personalities in a way that can make your family dynamic beautiful and wonderful. Your dreams may change and mature into something completely different than you thought they would be when you were younger. Life changes can happen so quickly. Finances won't always be what you hope them to be and can hinder the plans that you make for your life. Good decisions and poor decisions that you make individually or together as a couple can also shift life's path and carve out new roads.

The most important thing is to be unified as a couple. Communicate with each other. Make plans and decisions together. Be open and honest with each other about your feelings. If one of you really wants to do something, and the other feels uncomfortable about it, stop. Do not quickly make any big decisions that the other person is uncomfortable with. Take time to pray together. Listen for God's lead. Talk it through. Seek wise counsel. Then after you have done everything that you can to get on the same page, make a decision together.

Remember to continue dating even after you're married. Take time together away from life and away from responsibilities. Take time with friends and without friends. Continue to cultivate your friendship and continue to romance each other. Remember that there will be seasons of life where this isn't really possible, but try to get back to it as much as you can. For your marriage to remain strong, it is important to always be cultivating your relationship.

It won't always be easy, so as arguments and disagreements come up, you'll need to learn the rules of fighting fair.

Fighting Fair

In the previous chapters, I described all the things to watch out for that can be potentially damaging to your relationship. But, if your relationship only has minor issues, or issues that do not involve gaslighting or abuse, then the relationship still has potential. It may not be time to give it up yet.

Relationships are hard work, and there will be many times when you wonder if it's worth it. But, if you were both committed to making the relationship work, you will both learn and grow from each other and from each argument. You will need to learn how to listen to each other and validate each other's feelings. Sometimes you won't think that the other person is making any sense, but their feelings are real to them and should not be dismissed.

It's extremely important not to set unrealistic expectations on each other. Setting unrealistic expectations is bound to leave you disappointed. He is not you, and you are not him. You do not think the same way, even if there are a lot of similarities. He is not a mind reader. When you want a hug, you might need to ask for it. He might not be the kind of guy that thinks of it. He might be the kind of guy who needs space when he's angry so that he doesn't say something that he will regret. Learn to let him have his space and then come back together later and talk out the disagreement. Maybe you're on the other end of things. Maybe you're the one that needs time to cool down before you can have any kind of rational discussion. Make sure he understands that you still love him, but that you need some time to cool down before you can discuss the issue.

I am the kind of person that would rather hash it out right now and be done with it. My husband, however, is the kind that needs space first. For the first few years of marriage, we really didn't understand this about each other. We would get into an argument, and I would push and push trying to resolve the issue now. He would warn me that if I kept pushing that nothing productive was going to come out of his mouth. Since I didn't know how to stop pushing, he would end up having to leave the house. He would go for a drive, have the argument with me in his head, win the argument, and come back perfectly fine and ready to move on. I, however, had been sitting back at home waiting for him to come back so that we could resolve the issue and put it to rest. But, when he came back, he felt like the whole issue had been resolved! He had to learn that I also needed closure on our arguments. So, I learned to give him space, and he learned to give me closure. Now, we laugh at our immaturity, and share our stories with others so that they have a chance to learn more quickly than we did.

> *"As iron sharpens iron, so a man sharpens the countenance of his friend."*
> *Proverbs 21:17*

When someone is sharpening a knife, they will often use another knife and rub the two knives against each other. This smooths out any imperfections and sharpens both knives to make them more useful. God uses this analogy and Proverbs to show us that we need each other to help smooth out our own imperfections. He uses people that seemingly rub us the wrong way to sharpen us and make us more useful for the kingdom and strengthens our relationships with each other.

Persevering when a relationship gets tough is what makes a strong and lasting relationship. Without the determination to make the relationship work, it will fall apart. So, to fireproof your relationship, here are some things you need to remember when you are angry with each other.

1. You still love each other.
2. You are committed to this person.
3. Arguments and fights should become less severe and less frequent over time. It's completely normal to have arguments, but you should be learning and growing from them. If you find that you are still fighting a lot, it may be time to get some counseling from a trusted pastor or councilor.
4. Learn to fight fair. Try to take time to cool down before you discuss an issue. Never use absolutes "You never," "You always," and "Every Time," are extremely dangerous phrases to use in an argument. Instead, try using phrases that speak about how you feel. "I feel as though etc." or "when this happens, I feel etc."
5. Remember, it's not all about you! There are two people in this relationship. Both have valid feelings and good points most of the time. Make sure you listen to each other and try to understand where the other person is coming from.

In every aspect of life perseverance is important. Persevere when you are single and don't lower your standards. Persevere when you are dating and keep your boundaries strong. Guard your heart and guard your future husband's heart. Persevere when you're married. Work through disagreements and differences together so that you can build a unified life that others can look to for inspiration.

Love Never Fails

Chapter 17

Verb 'Will never break down or cease to work well.'

My Story

In the months and years that followed, I was hit with the full impact of why it is so important to save yourself for marriage. Frankie and I have gone through many difficulties before we were married. I could not imagine trying to deal with all of the pre-marriage issues along with all of the early marriage issues. Waiting to get married and abstaining from sex had not only given us time to work through personality differences without added physical connection, but the sexual tension between us had given us a chance to see some of the "ugly" sides of each other and decide if we were still willing to push through.

We have been married for over a decade now. And our marriage has only gotten stronger over time. We've seen victories and defeats. We've seen gains and losses. We've had the joy of having children, the grief of a miscarriage and the devastation of losing my parents and his father over the period of several years. We've even experienced the great blessing of being able to restore a precious piece of Frankie's past that could have been lost forever. A shining light of God's grace and mercy when it is so deeply undeserved. I am a full-time-mom and homeschool our kids. Frankie is a pastor now, and I'm fully blessed to be working alongside him in ministry.

We still have our disagreements. After all, we are still individuals with different personalities and opinions. But, when it's all said and done, one thing remains. God's faithfulness to us as we keep our focus on Him. He is still first in each of our lives, and we work at making him first in our marriage too. We trust Him to show us how to raise these children to love Him and serve Him. Because we know His love never fails us.

God Never Fails

"Fear not, for I am with you; be not dismayed, for I am your God; I will strengthen you, I will help you, I will uphold you with my righteous right hand."
Isaiah 41:10

God's promise is that He will always be with you. There is nothing you can do, no evil you can commit that can change how much He loves you and wants to have a relationship with you. You can't run far enough, dig deep enough or fly high enough to be out of His loving gaze. There is nothing in this world that can happen to you that can separate you from Him... no matter how bad it was. He was there. He felt your pain and hurt with you. He saw you through it and strengthened you despite it.

If you've gone through a tragedy or someone did something horrific to you, you may say, "If God was there, why didn't He stop it?" It's a very good question. The hard reality is that because of Adam & Eve's sin, the world is corrupt. God, in His sovereignty, gave us free will to choose good or evil, life or death, love or hate. He did this so that it would be our choice to have a relationship with Him or not. If He didn't give us a choice, it wouldn't be real love. We would be robots just doing God's bidding.

However, whenever faced with the temptation to sin, He did say that He would always provide a better option. A different choice that would help us to avoid sin.

> *"No temptation has overtaken you except such as is common to man; but God is faithful, who will not allow you to be tempted beyond what you are able, but with the temptation will also make the way of escape, that you may be able to bear it."*
> *I Corinthians 10:13*

Unfortunately, many people choose evil. Many people choose to hurt themselves or each other. God is a just God, and each person will account for their own sin and the evil they have done to others, but He will not take away our free will.

No matter what you go through in life, no matter what has happened in your past, no matter what you struggle with now or in the future, God can turn every bad decision and every ugly circumstance into something beautiful and amazing. All you need to do is turn to Him and surrender your will to His. He will not fail you.

> *"And we know that all things work together for good to those who love God, to those who are called according to His purpose".*
> *Romans 8:28*

His love never fails. His love will never let you down. His love will pick you up from the ashes and set you on solid ground. His love will help you to build an incredible and fulfilling life. Not necessarily a life filled with money and things (although He does promise to provide for our needs), but a life filled with love, community, and connection. A life worth fighting for.

> *"But seek first the kingdom of God*
> *and His righteousness,*
> *and all these things shall be added to you."*
> *Matthew 6:33*

Happily Ever After? Fail Proofing Your Relationship

"We've fallen out of love." Is a phrase I hear way too often. To put it bluntly, this is a cop out. It's an excuse for not wanting to try anymore. It's a weakness that does not belong in a relationship. People do not "fall out of love" any more than they "fall into love." A better way to say it may be "We don't have affection for each other and are bored with our relationship" or "It's become too hard, and we don't want to keep trying to make our relationship work."

In fact, I recently heard something that got me thinking about dating from a different perspective. Again, I am not against dating, but this is interesting food for thought. The idea is that dating is supposed to be trying relationships out until you find the right person, but the more you date the more practice you get breaking up and the more comfortable you are with the idea of divorce. You spend much time investing in and getting to know someone until you decide that the relationship has become too hard or isn't what you wanted, so, you just end it. The danger here is that when you finally decide to invest in a marriage and build a life together you are already in a pre-learned habit of getting out when things get hard or uncomfortable.

Real love doesn't give up when things get hard. Real love sticks together through the good times and the bad, for better or for worse, in sickness and in health, to love and to cherish until death do you part. There's a reason those phrases are included in "traditional wedding vows." These words have been around for generations because marriage has largely been looked on as a permanent decision that two people make.

In recent years, marriage has become more of a "piece of paper," an excuse for a wedding, or a convenient way to live together. Real commitment seems to be completely missing from over half of marriages. Do you really want your marriage to be as meaningless as a piece of paper? Or do you want a marriage that will last forever? Are you willing to wait and search for a man who will be committed to your relationship and your marriage until death do you part? If you are, commit the words of I Corinthians 13 to memory and put them into practice. Look for a godly man who will put God first and you second. Be a committed follower of Jesus and learn from his teachings. Let Him write your love story. I promise that it's worth the wait.

> *"... For this reason, a man will leave his father and mother and be united to his wife, and the two will become one flesh."*
> *Ephesians 5:30-31*

I do not believe God intends for us to disown our families once we start one of our own. I believe what He's doing here is helping us to understand that when we get married, our marriage and our new family need to become the top priority when it comes to earthly relationships. Our dependence is no longer on our parents, and while we still have the responsibility to honor them, we are no longer to put our relationships and our obligations with our birth families first. He asks us to do this so that we can truly focus on our relationship with our spouse and learn how to do life and responsibility together. Don't worry, He never said you shouldn't call your mom and dad for advice. They can still give you guidance. After all, they've had a lot more life experience than you!

> *"Now as the church submits to Christ,
> so also wives should submit
> to their husbands in everything.
> Husbands, love your wives, just as Christ loved the church
> and gave Himself up for her."*
> *Ephesians 5:24-25*

"Woah, wait just a minute! Are you saying I'm Supposed to submit to my husband?!"

Yes, you read that right. We are supposed to submit to our husbands in the way that we submit to God (unless submitting to your husband means going against God's laws). But don't worry. God doesn't leave it at that. There is a balance to every good marriage. Our husbands are to love us the same way that Christ loved the church! The kindness that God has shown us is the same kindness we are to look for in a husband. God doesn't expect us to submit to just anyone. He wants us to find someone who loves HIM with all his heart so that he has the capability of loving you the way that God does. He is to love you in such a way that your wellbeing is his top priority. This means everything from providing for your needs to caring for your emotions. You see, just as women desire to be cherished, God designed men to desire respect. Both are beautiful forms of love that should be shown between husband and wife. If we're giving respect to our husbands, it makes it easy for him to love and cherish us...and if our husbands love us properly, we will have no problem respecting them. If either party is failing in one of these areas, the relationship will be off balance. That doesn't necessarily mean the relationship should end, but that you both need to work at restoring balance together. Talk things out and pray together. If that doesn't work, seek counsel from a godly resource.

> *"...submitting to one another in the fear of God."*
> *Ephesians 5:22*

Let me also explain that submitting to our husbands in no way means that wives don't have a voice or that their opinions aren't valid or valuable. We've already covered what that mindset can do to a relationship. When a husband is leading properly, he will highly value the perspective and wisdom that his wife has to offer. The Bible is clear that this isn't a "man is more important than woman" kind of thing. God is clear throughout the Bible that very human is just as valued and important. Regardless of gender, race, skin color, status, possessions, clothing, or belief system.

Sometimes, our husbands will acquiesce to us because they can see that we are right in certain situations. Sometimes, we will realize that he is correct and follow his lead. Decisions (especially big ones) should be made together. After all, decisions in a marriage don't just affect the husband or the wife. They affect the entire family. When done correctly, both parties will feel valued, validated, and content in an equal respect partnership.

"Now that I understand what love is, how do I become a Keyper?"

I hope that after reading this book you've decided that purity of mind and body are an important part of who you want to be. Being a Keyper means much more than just making a commitment to save sex for marriage, it's also deciding to be careful what you watch, listen to, do, and what company you. Being a Keyper means cultivating a pure heart as a lifelong adventure to explore either alone or with the spouse God brings along.

I hope that you make a decision to be pure while you are still a virgin and save yourself a lot of heartache. But remember this, a Keyper can make the decision at any stage of their life. Pre-teen to adult, single parent, married, or divorced. The important thing here is to make a commitment to God that you are going to maintain purity in your heart, in your life, and in your relationships. The goal is to trust that God really and truly does have your best interests at heart and will not let you down. He will either bring along the right person for you in His perfect time, help you to become pure in your current relationship, or He will give you the strength and even the desire to be single and serve Him without a spouse.

Whatever you decide, please know and understand that God loves you and is here for you every moment of your life. He is only a breath away and He will not fail you.

Made in the USA
Columbia, SC
28 July 2024